MAT TALES

True Stories from the Bizarre, Brutal World of Pro Boxing

DAN SISNEROS

Editor: Bob McLain
Layout: Artisanal Text

ISBN 978-1-68390-104-4
Printed in the United States of America

Pulp Hero Press | www.PulpHeroPress.com
Address queries to bob@pulpheropress.com

Contents

Foreword

The 15th and final round begins. Your trainer says, "Throw a right to the body and a left to the head." Your co-trainer says, "Mike, your mother is crying." Your manager says, "You can only win if you knock him out!" and you are sitting on the stool reciting the 23rd Psalm and asking the Lord to "Give me the strength to knock him out, like I believe you said I would." The bell rings, you get going, and all of a sudden, *he's down*!

The ref is counting and you are saying, "Oh Lord, don't let that bell ring before he says 10." You hear him say it—"10!" Suddenly, I think I am a gymnast as the excitement fills me. I try a flip right in the middle of the ring, and I realize I am *not* a gymnast. I say, "Oh well, I messed up. So what, I am the new heavyweight world champion! I'll just lay down taking it all in 'till my cornermen come and lift me up." What an amazing feeling it was. That is what happened when I won the heavyweight title against John Tate.

Yeah, that's crazy and great. But boxing is also crazy in a not-so-great way—like when you've trained for eight years to reach your dream, and people who are against you take that away in 63 seconds. That happened to me in my third title defense when I met Michael Dokes for the first time.

Boxing is a crazy game. Imagine, I had to knock a man out cold in the 15th round, watching him fall face first and laying still on the canvas to win the title. Then I had it taken from me in 63 seconds, barely enough time to get warmed up, standing there fighting back, and the referee just comes over, breaks us, grabs the other man's wrist, and raises his arm as the new champion.

Dan's book is full of crazy things like that, and I know they happen. I've LIVED them!

Mike Weaver
Former WBA Heavyweight World Champion

Introduction

Boxing has been called many things by many people. The "sweet science," the "theater of the unexpected," a "blood sport," brutal and beautiful. Those monikers are all correct. Its history is rich. American heroes have been made in the ring, as well as villains, champions, scoundrels, role models, social misfits, eloquent ambassadors of the sport. Boxing has it all. It appeals to the man on the street, and it is like a magnet for the rich and famous. Tune in to any big-time boxing event on television, and you will see stars scattered throughout the crowd, placed as close to the front as possible by the promoters to bring color and importance to the event. Behind them, all the way up into the rafters against the walls, are the common boxing fans who may have had to save up just to be there. They make up the crowd, and they get their money's worth with loud cheering. Most come to see their favorite fighters in action. Some are just glad to have a chance to experience the spectacle live and in person. Me? These days, I enjoy sitting in the comfort of my living room with my favorite people, eating peanuts out of the shell, popcorn, sipping on a Coke Zero, and taking it all in—analyzing every round, second guessing the trainers and the officials. It's just fun.

For about a decade, I had the honor of being one of those officials who get second guessed. Not much criticism came my way, but I had my moments. Like the time I was the lone judge who scored the bout 97-94 in favor of Frankie Swindell over Samson Po'uha in their first meeting on April 5, 1997, fought in Albuquerque and carried on Fox Sports. The other judges scored the fight 98-93 and 95-94 in favor of Po'uha. Fox Sports broadcasters Barry Tompkins and Rich Marotta both had the fight scored in favor of Samson Po'uha. When the scores were read, a cheer went up from the crowd as my score in favor of Swindell was read, but Tompkins, Marotta, and the other two judges had it in favor of Po'uha. Swindell felt he won clearly and shook his head in disgust. Fans came out of the audience to tell me I was the only one who got it right. I felt certain in my scorecard, and even getting scolded by Po'uha's manager didn't change that certainty.

I've watched that fight maybe five times since then on videotape. I'm still sure I got it right, at least from where I was sitting. But that's boxing. In the post-fight interview, the winner, Samson Po'uha, said that he "gambled, and drew 21." Barry Tompkins made the remark "If you ask Swindell, he'll say it was craps." It was close enough. I would not say that the broadcasters or the other two judges got it wrong. They called it as they saw it. No argument from me. Tompkins was inducted into the International Boxing Hall of Fame in 2017. Rich Marotta is a member of the California Boxing Hall of Fame. These two hall of famers didn't see the fight the way I did. And they said so on national TV. It's just fun.

A fun blood sport. Sounds strange, doesn't it? People have been killed in the ring, badly injured, and that is nothing to laugh about. People's lives have been changed, ruined, even taken in the ring. All in the name of sport? But I have always defended that sport. I never saw it as representing hatred or evil. I saw it as sport. The deeper I got into it, the more I could see through the built-up pre-fight "hatred" between the two fighters. No matter how much was said, how ugly the remarks, after the fight the two would usually shake hands and hug each other after a brutal war. Danny Romero vs. Johnny Tapia is a perfect example. That one was built up to be a certain riot. They even had to change venues due to all of the fears generated by the pre-fight hype. Some of it was genuine, but within a few weeks, I heard nothing but respect from each fighter about the other. That's what I saw in the sport.

Before becoming so deeply involved in boxing, I used to tune in to fights on TV and sometimes yell, "Kill him!" or "Kill that bum!" I was quite naïve. It was not until I sat up against the ring as a judge that I saw the danger, the seriousness of the action, the potential for harm. It changed the way I saw things—but not for the worse, for the better. I had a deeper respect for the boxers that were putting everything they had on the line, in front of hundreds, thousands, even millions of critical eyes. I used to call fighters "bums" if they had more losses than wins, or if they were on a big losing streak. That changed, too. There are no bums in boxing. I understand that the term is thrown around, not to personally degrade any fighter, but to categorize them as someone who is supposed to lose, or someone who is looked upon as an underdog in a particular bout. But to me it is the "B" word, and I don't like it anymore. If I catch myself using that word, it is a rare occasion, but when I'm aware of the "B" word slipping out of my mouth, it is generic, saying that someone fought "a bunch of bums," but I will never call any fighter a bum.

Boxing does have its truly fun side, too. It really does! Comical, colorful, exciting, something that the sport's fans love to share. There is controversy around every corner in boxing as well. Ring announcers' styles, referees' judgments, judges' scorecards. The unexpected from fans, fighters, officials, broadcasters, and all of the people who make this sport the grand spectacle it is. But most fights don't take place at Thomas & Mack Arena in Las Vegas, Nevada, or Madison Square Garden in New York City. Most fights are at the local convention center, a community college gymnasium, or even a roller rink. I've attended fights at most of the above. The unexpected things that happen at the smaller venues hardly ever get mentioned, but if every hard-core boxing fan was asked, they would share some doozies. If you are involved in this sport long enough, in any capacity, even as a fan, you will sooner or later encounter something incredible.

I would like to share with you some crazy moments from the sport of boxing. Some of my friends from the sport—fellow boxing historians, writers, boxers, trainers, even the former chairman of the New York State Athletic Commission—will also share their recollections of what they felt and thought as they witnessed these unusual events unfolding before their eyes. Many are from nationally televised events, some are from the local boxing scene where I officiated during the 1990s. Others you may have seen, especially if you are a boxing fan like myself, and I hope it will bring on a reaction of "Oh yeah, I remember that!" and maybe a bit of a smile will appear, or a shake of the head. And for the events that you are hearing about for the first time, I pass them on to you as I witnessed them.

I do hope you will keep in mind that I'm just the messenger. If you have been mentioned in this book, don't take it as an insult, because it is not. You have become a small part of boxing history, and be assured, I have the utmost respect for every person spoken of in these accounts. Maybe you found yourself in the wrong place at the wrong time, or you were the victim of an equipment failure, or lacked access to today's technology (like instant video replay). Maybe you made a bad choice, or lost self-control. Maybe you're just misunderstood. Or maybe you were the judge on the wrong side of a nationally televised split decision whose scorecard was questioned by a hall-of-fame broadcaster on national TV. I don't share these true tales with the intent of making fun of anyone, but I also know that we are *all* human, and I don't think any sport brings that out of us like boxing does. Laugh, or shake your head, but remember ... there are no bums in boxing!

Dan Sisneros
Las Cruces, New Mexico

CHAPTER ONE

No Time Outs in Boxing

Donald Curry vs. James Green

March 30, 1985
Dallas, Texas

The bout was televised live on ABC's *Wide World of Sports* and featured red-hot unbeaten welterweight world champion Donald Curry in a non-title bout against a tough and respected contender, James "Hard Rock" Green, in a bout scheduled for 10 rounds in the junior middleweight division.

Curry held the IBF and WBA welterweight title belts. This bout was considered a "stay sharp" bout as he was looking down the road to a showdown of unbeaten welterweight champions against WBC king Milton McCrory. Curry's name was also being mentioned as a possible challenger in what would be a mega-bout against the winner of the Marvin Hagler / Thomas Hearns fight. It was also a "test" bout as the fight was contested at the 154 lb. junior middleweight limit, and was Curry's first time moving seven pounds north. Before the fight, Curry said he was struggling to make the 147 lb. weight limit, and wanted to test the waters at 154. Green was considered only a slight threat to Curry, but with his 20–4, 13 KO record, and being a natural 154-pounder, some fight fans saw the threat as quite a bit more than *slight*. Green's four losses came to world-class opponents: three in the junior middleweight division, and one was at the 160 lb. middleweight class to world-ranked Frank "The Animal" Fletcher.

At only 5'4" tall, Green had a 5-inch disadvantage in height to the 5'9" Curry, and a 5" reach disadvantage, too. Those numbers were nothing new for Green, who adopted a style similar to heavyweight champion Joe Frazier that was effective against the taller fighters he usually faced. Donald Curry was a stand-up boxer with a classic style and paralyzing power in both hands. He was considered one of the top "pound-for-pound" fighters in the world.

Local favorite Curry did a good job of controlling the aggressive Green in the first round. Professional boxing referee and judge Woody Kislowski recalls how the bout itself was shaping up:

> **Kislowski**: Round 1 was somewhat competitive, although Donald Curry had the clear edge. Curry was sharp, landing with jabs and the uppercut. Green threw an ineffective jab and did land a couple of combinations, but didn't press the action as he should have.

With some good exchanges to start round 2, everything came to a halt at about 40 seconds into the round as a retreating Green was caught with a straight left from Curry. Green began making a motion with his right hand over his eye causing Curry to cease his attack and walk away. Referee Dick Cole stepped in and immediately began waving his right hand in the air to call a halt to the bout.

> **Kislowski**: In the first minute of round 2, following a nice flurry underneath by Green, Curry landed a jab, missed with another, then threw one more jab followed by a right hand that inadvertently thumbed Green who immediately reacted to it. Donald landed one more punch and then stopped throwing for a second and walked away as Green was dealing with the thumb. Referee Dickie Cole, who later became the Texas commissioner, immediately stepped in and waved it off. Green protested, saying that he was thumbed, but Dickie said to him, "You don't have any time outs". As "Hard Rock" Green walked off in disgust, Lou Duva came in and went crazy all over Cole as only Captain Lou could do, but to no avail.

The ABC microphones picked up the exchange. The referee then walked over to Curry and grabbed his left arm, raising his hand in victory, angering Green, and bringing an enraged Lou

Duva into the ring to aggressively question Cole's decision. With hands flailing in the air, Duva continued to question Cole about what had just happened. Cole remained calm, and stood in the corner as Duva's grievances continued. Again, the ABC microphones picked up some of the conversation:

Cole: He quit fighting, he quit fighting.

Duva: The guy walked away, the guy WALKED AWAY!

Cole: He should have went down to one knee.

Duva: Why? Why go down to one? OH, COME ON!

Cole: Because I can't stop a fight.

Duva: You can't stop a fight like that!

Cole: No, if he can't fight, I can stop the fight.

The ring announcer made it official: a technical knockout at 48 seconds of round 2, leading ABC commentator Al Michaels to say:

Michaels: Frankly, my initial impression is that Cole stopped it much too early...

Initially, it looked like Green had pulled away after being hit with a straight left hand from Curry, but the slow-motion replay showed that it was a right uppercut just before that left hand which had unintentionally caught Green in the eye with a thumb, causing him to retreat and take the straight left.

The Curry crowd was booing as controversy and confusion filled the ring. From a distance, the fans may have felt that Green just quit. A fan could be heard yelling, "Now let 'em fight for REAL now!"

James Green went over to Curry to explain things from his side, which did not sit well with the frustrated Donald Curry. It was easy to read his lips as he said, "I didn't thumb you!".

Curry took the microphone from the ring announcer and told the crowd "I'm sorry, but I am not the referee".

Al Michaels and the ABC broadcast crew tried to get things sorted out after the bout. Curry was asked about it, and he said that he did not feel that he had thumbed Green.

Referee Dick Cole had a chance to explain what happened when Michaels asked him why the fight was stopped:

> **Cole**: I had no choice, I had to stop the fight. Green was not defending himself. I think Green got hit with a left jab, and it hit him and he got his eye and impaired his vision. Curry stepped back, and like a gentleman, he did not take advantage of him. But, if I let the fight go on, Curry was going to come in and nail him.
>
> **Michaels**: Did Green contend that he was thumbed, or that he was just hit?
>
> **Cole**: Well, he contended that he was thumbed, but if I don't see a thumb, I can't call it.
>
> **Michaels**: Was there any thought in your mind of waving them, at least, back together to attempt to give them the opportunity to continue on?
>
> **Cole**: He did not attempt to try to defend himself. You know, Curry hit him with a short right hand ... after he started, to throw his hands up ... and said his eye was, you know, felt his eye.
>
> **Michaels**: Now, under the rules here in the state of Texas, what are you to do in a situation like that, what does it say to do?
>
> **Cole**: If a man is not defending hisself, I have to stop the fight. If we had a standing 8-count, I could have given him a standing 8-count. We have no standing 8-count in Texas. If he had thought, he would have dropped to one knee, then I could have given him an 8-count, but he didn't drop to one knee, and I can't force him to one knee.

They then reviewed slow-motion footage together, but didn't seem to catch the right uppercut that caused the unintentional thumbing.

Cole made a gracious final statement after being asked:

> **Michaels**: Right now, are you satisfied that you definitely made *the* right decision?
>
> **Cole**: I made the only decision I could make.
>
> **Michaels**: And so, even if you could do it all over again, having seen what you just saw, knowing how people feel at the moment, you would have done it?

> **Cole**: I'm sorry the bout turned out the way it did, but I had no choice, I had to stop the fight.

Green was brought in to be asked about what happened. He expressed being hurt by the way things ended after training so hard for this fight. He said that the uppercut was indeed the punch that brought the thumb into the eye, causing Green to back up when everything "went blurry." Green's trainer, Lou Duva, pleaded his fighter's case very clearly:

> **Duva**: Give a mandatory 8-count, it's at the discretion of the referee, and what he says is why didn't he go down? He didn't have to go down, there's a mandatory 8-count in effect, and if he thought that he was hurt, why didn't he give him a standing 8-count? That's all. If he thought he was hurt. But all he did was complain about the thumb in the eye. I mean, it's a weird ending, and its just too bad because James is mentally and physically OK. It's not the right thing to do for boxing, not the right thing to do for the public, and the television people out there, he wanted to fight, he came to fight. He wanted to get over the first couple of rounds, and then open right up. I mean the people were deprived of a good fight. A discretionary call ... whether it's ball and strike, but for me, nobody can tell me that there wasn't something wrong with that there. He got a thumb in the eye, and you got a thumb in the eye, where do you stop a fight on a thumb in the eye?
>
> **Michaels**: So you think he acted too quickly? What precipitates action like that?
>
> **Duva**: Absolutely, he over-reacted. Over-reaction. He over-reacted. If he wanted to do something he could have given ... if he wanted to do something, if he thought he was in danger of being hurt, he could have given a mandatory 8-count, and then at that time take a look at him, and then make his discretion up, whether he could continue or not, that's what he could have done.

Again, Green expressed how he was tired of "getting the short end of the stick," even hinting that he might not fight again. Duva did say that he thought Cole was still a good referee, but repeated his frustration with the final decision. Woody Kislowski looks at it from a referee's point of view:

> **Kislowski:** I'll never publicly criticize another referee as it is a very difficult job where you have to make split-second decisions and you literally hold a boxer's life in your hands, but I will simply say that if it had been me in that particular situation, unless I could see something from being right up close that Dickie did and I couldn't see as an observer from outside of the ring, I wouldn't have stopped the fight then. I can see why there was an outcry, but again, only the referee is that close in and he has a unique perspective that even the ringside judges don't have, so I have no criticism of Dickie.

James Green would go on to fight nine more times, going 2–5–2 in that final stretch. He was still highly regarded and faced off with some high level contenders, ending his career with a North American Boxing Federation middleweight title challenge against Otis Grant.

Donald Curry would continue his storied career, two fights later winning a unification showdown bout against WBC champion Milton McCrory with a spectacular 2nd round knockout. He would go on to fight at a world-class level for 12 more years.

This was a classic crossroads fight with a very strange ending. In the final analysis, referee Dick Cole could not call what he did not see (the thumb from the uppercut), and the confusion over a "standing" 8-count vs. a "mandatory" 8-count contributed to the turmoil. But it made for some entertaining boxing drama.

CHAPTER TWO

The Second Time Around

Vito Antuefermo vs. Marvin Hagler II

June 13, 1981
Boston, Massachusetts

Marvin Hagler had campaigned for 6½ years before getting his first chance at a world title. When finally he did, he faced defending champion Vito Antuefermo at Caesar's Palace in Las Vegas. It was a grueling battle that ended in a 15-round split draw, with Antuefermo retaining his title.

Hagler ran off three straight wins against world-ranked opposition, and won the undisputed middleweight world title with a third-round stoppage of defending champion Alan Minter in London. After an eighth-round stoppage over unbeaten Fulgencio Obelmejias (30–0) in his first title defense, Hagler was set to defend his title in a rematch with Vito Antuefermo, on his home turf—Boston Garden.

It was a highly anticipated event as Marvin Hagler felt he had clearly won the first meeting. Antuefermo badly wanted to regain his title belt. Vito had a reputation as a bleeder, and just 30 seconds into the first round, the two banged heads causing a profuse cut to the left side of the challenger's forehead. Though it appeared that Antuefermo was the one who instigated the butt, his head trainer, Freddie Brown, went nuts and climbed up onto the ring apron to yell at referee Davey Pearl. The referee showed restraint as he could have taken away a point, or even disqualified the challenger for the actions of his trainer, but Pearl just signaled Freddie Brown to get back down off of the apron. When the bell sounded to end round 1, Antuefermo's corner went to work trying to stop that cut.

Brown made the motion with his hands that the fight was over. He insisted that Hagler butted his man, and walked over to the commissioners of the Massachusetts Boxing Commission, with his chief second, Panama Lewis, to plead their case. It was a confusing scene, as the bell had sounded for round 2 of this world-championship bout, but the arguing continued, turning a one-minute interval between rounds into three full minutes. The champion, Hagler, stood at the ready the entire time while the officials sorted out the chaos. Fight trainer and cutman Dan Cushner remembers it well:

> **Cushner**: Vito Antuofermo had a face that was a cutman's nightmare. He probably started bleeding when he signed the contract for the rematch with Hagler. Just 45 seconds into the first round, Vito suffered the first of many cuts in this fight. The cause of the cut was an unintentional headbutt on his hairline. Any time a boxer is cut near the scalp, the bleeding is immense. When the bell rang ending the first round, Vito's face was a crimson mess. Vito's head trainer, Freddie Brown, complained to the referee that Hagler should be disqualified. The rest time far exceeded the normal one minute after that first round. One of two things happened: either Vito's corner was stalling for more time for the coagulant to set up, or Vito's corner was saying that he couldn't continue because of the cut and wanted the fight to be declared a no-contest or a technical draw since four rounds had not been completed. Vito's corner seemed confused and not too sure of the aforementioned rulings and allowed Vito to continue the fight.

Promoter Bob Arum yelled at the commissioners to clear everyone out of the ring and resume the fight. Brown relented, and the bell rang to start the second round. The battle continued and was fierce. As the bell sounded to end the round, the boxers glared at each other before walking back to their corners.

Hagler smartly began targeting the gash on the head, landing a left hand that put Antuefermo on the deck. He got up quickly and didn't appear to be badly hurt. The battle continued, but it was Hagler looking like a machine and remaining in control of the action.

Southpaw Hagler continued to sting his opponent with hard right jabs and hard left hands, opening a cut over the right eye of Antuefermo. As the bell sounded to end round 4, Antuefermo sat on his stool with a red mask, as both sides of his face were now leaking blood.

Again, Antuefermo's trainer Freddie Brown raised a ruckus, threatening to not let the fight continue and demanding that Hagler should be disqualified. Referee Davey Pearl finally had enough of the drama, walked over to Marvin Hagler, grabbed his arm, and raised his hand as the winner.

> **Cushner**: While headbutts are a common occurrence when fighting a southpaw, this fight had more than normal due to each boxer's style. Vito was slightly shorter and would come in with his head down and Hagler would lower his head to start his combinations by hitting the body first. Vito began taking hard punches from Hagler and a straight left knocked him down in the fourth round. By the end of the round, Vito's face was cut in several places and the fight was stopped. In my opinion, Hagler was too much for Vito and would have stopped him in another round or two. Their first fight ended in a controversial draw as Hagler won the early rounds and Vito came back to win the later rounds. Hagler started this fight much faster and was in control until the stoppage.

When Hagler walked over to say something to Antuefermo, Freddie Brown started barking at him. Hagler's trainers smartly dragged him back to his corner before things could escalate. It was bloody, it was down and dirty, but it was Marvin Hagler who remained champion, and felt he had righted a wrong decision that was given in their first meeting.

> **Cushner**: Vito's corner should have claimed that he could not continue after the first round due to the headbutt. It would have been a bad decision for the fans, but Vito would have been awarded another nice payday versus Hagler.

Vito Antuefermo would fight just five more times, never earning another shot at the world title. Hagler made nine more successful defenses of his titles and earned boxing immortality.

CHAPTER THREE

Takin' It to the Street

Trevor Berbick vs. Larry Holmes Street Brawl

April 8, 1991
Hollywood, Florida

Larry Holmes and Trevor Berbick met for the WBC heavyweight title in 1981. Holmes defended his title easily, nearly sweeping all three judges' scorecards. Ten years later, they met again, and it seems Holmes won once more—but he was not defending a title. This battle took place out on the street in front of the Diplomat hotel in Hollywood, Florida. Boxing writer/historian Vernon Gravely remembers what happened that evening very well:

> **Gravely**: In an episode of *The Simpsons* that aired in the early 1990s, Lisa made a comment about Homer's favorite sport, wrestling. Homer immediately corrected her: "It's boxing, Lisa. There's a world of difference." For anyone who's ever witnessed the "street brawl" between former heavyweight champions Larry Holmes and Trevor Berbick, the shenanigans exhibited by the fighters demonstrated a world where boxing and wrestling shared more similarities than differences.

After easily disposing of Tim Anderson in one round. Larry Holmes held a post-fight press conference, and was asked about offering a rematch to Trevor Berbick. Holmes didn't take the challenge very seriously and left the dais.

> **Gravely**: Berbick was in attendance at that press conference. Holmes said that he didn't respect Berbick, he didn't like his attitude, and he had already beaten him decisively, winning fifteen rounds of their 1981

> fifteen-rounder. Immediately following this statement, Holmes paused, then said, "Maybe he won one round."

Berbick then began raving about Holmes messing up his married life, and some other incoherent rantings. It was a crazy scene that made most of the press-conference attendees a bit uncomfortable.

> **Gravely**: Shortly thereafter, Holmes left the room, at which point Berbick went on a profanity-laden, barely-coherent tirade about "Jenny from Jacksonville" and Larry Holmes' efforts to destroy his [Berbick's] family life. "All the problems I have are through him," Berbick stated. More problems were soon to come. Although Holmes wasn't in the room to hear the rant, his wife was, and when she got word to her hubby about Berbick's disrespectful comments, Larry got pissed.

Later, the two began to scuffle as witnesses say that Larry Holmes ran out to the front of the hotel and began kicking and punching Berbick who was still ranting about something.

> **Gravely**: When the cameras next caught up with Berbick, he was outside the hotel, a police officer on either side, shouting that he had just been accosted by Larry Holmes. For a man who, moments before, had claimed he would "break all his ribs in his body" if he got into a street fight with Holmes, Berbick looked like someone who had been on the losing end. Maybe Holmes had just taken him by surprise? Probably. And he was about to do it again.

Video cameras started rolling as Berbick, dressed in a dark pin-striped suit, was dusty and mussed up, began yelling to everyone that "Larry Holmes kicked me and punched me!" Seconds later, as Berbick was telling his story to police and reporters out on the sidewalk, an angry Larry Holmes came running across the top of a parked limousine, dressed in his stylish white sweats and street shoes, and leapt off of the vehicle with a two-legged drop kick that any Mexican luchador would be proud of. The 41-year-old Holmes landed solid on the torso of Berbick and continued to brawl with him until police broke it up.

> **Gravely**: When Holmes tackled Berbick, the two of them and a police officer ended up on the ground. About half a dozen police officers rushed in to pull Holmes off of everybody.

There were no arrests made for this incident. The whole scene had the feel of a pro wrestling event, but there was nothing scripted about the damage that Berbick suffered.

> **Gravely**: Holmes managed to go 3–0 in his first night back as a professional fighter, and he didn't suffer so much as one broken rib.

Larry Holmes fought for eleven more years after taking Berbick to the ground, going 20–3 from that point with the three losses all being for title belts.

Berbick went 12–4 after the incident, fighting for two minor title belts and winning the Canadian heavyweight title. He was found dead in a church parking lot in 2006. His 21-year-old nephew was convicted of the murder along with a 19-year-old accomplice.

CHAPTER FOUR

My First Boxing Riot

Anthony Chavez vs. Rudy Lovato

March 19, 1993
Albuquerque, New Mexico

With seven local favorites on a five-bout card held at Roller West, a roller rink converted into an event hall for the night, there were bound to be some grudge matches.

The one that captured the imaginations of the fans in attendance featured two Albuquerque fighters. Anthony Chavez was fighting in his home town for only the second time in eight bouts. He was hungry for his first win, and it could not be any sweeter than to get it against "Bad Boy" Rudy Lovato, also an Albuquerque favorite, and who had been a champion kickboxer before going "hands only" for pay. The match looked even on paper, with both boxers in their ninth professional fight.

According to Louie Burke, a member of the New Mexico State Athletic Commission at the time, there was a rivalry between the gyms, but nobody in any official capacity thought it was intense enough to not approve the match:

> **Burke**: We knew there was some animosity, but didn't know how much. You know, home town, Albuquerque, that kind of thinking. We really did not expect any kind of trouble or we would have made sure to have more security.

I asked Rudy Lovato—the man in the center of the storm—if there was bad blood involved:

> **Lovato**: No, there was never any bad blood going into the fight, it was just more of the heat-of-the-moment thing. During the fight, I realized it got out of control once I seen everybody running up and jumping into the ring.

Lovato entered the ring playing to his "Bad Boy" image with a backwards baseball cap, sunglasses, and a black/white serape. In his corner was light-heavyweight hall-of-fame world champion Bob Foster, assisted by Lorenzo White. Chavez entered the ring in the most basic of styles: black trunks, no hat, no robe, no spectacle, just here to fight. In his corner was boxing trainer Henry Anaya Sr., assisted by fellow New Mexican Paul Chavez, the original trainer of the great Johnny Tapia.

I worked the card that night, but was not assigned to this particular bout. The assigned judges were Rocky Burke, Sandy Pino, and Neffie Quintana. Merv Nephew drew the referee assignment for this one. He had four years of experience as a professional referee, and would need every minute of it on this night.

The fight started off looking like it was going to be a well-matched battle. It was scheduled for six rounds, but wouldn't even make it halfway there. Lovato started with a stick-and-move method, navigating around the outside of the ring using his jab and lots of foot movement. Chavez took command of the center of the ring and tried to catch Lovato with power punches. It was about one minute into the fight when Lovato got a warning for a kidney punch from the referee. Lovato continued to shoot out his jab keeping Chavez at bay, and tying Chavez up every time he felt pressure. It looked like a bout that could go the distance, and would possibly depend on the stamina of the two boxers.

As the bell sounded to end the first round, Lovato "bumped" Chavez on his way back to the corner. Chavez took exception to that gesture and turned around to go after Lovato, but was held back and ordered to go to his corner by the referee.

Chavez came out for the second round looking a little more intent on doing some damage by trying to follow every jab with a hard right hand. Lovato continued with his slashing style, sticking Chavez with that jab and moving all around the ring, the white tassels on his shoes bouncing with every step. It was a good, even fight. Chavez would land a few solid uppercuts inside, and Lovato would answer with flashy combinations.

As the bell sounded to end the second round, Lovato was right in the middle of a combination of punches, and he didn't stop at the sound of the bell. Chavez fired back, and the two went into all-out fighting mode with referee Merv Nephew doing all he could to break the two apart. Foster and White jumped into the ring to try and get a hold of Lovato and bring him back to the corner, while Henry Anaya Sr. jumped in and tried to pull Chavez out of the mix. The crowd was going wild, and since it was such an intimate setting for a boxing venue, they were feeling like part of the action. Soon, some of them *became* part of the action!

The two boxers went back to their corners thinking that the bout would continue in round 3, but Nephew went over to the commissioners' table and bent down to announce, "The blue corner [Chavez] is disqualified!" Not everyone knew what had been determined, and the round girl entered with her big "3" card walking around the ring announcing the start of round 3. Ring announcer Leroy Mora was introducing the girl, and it seemed like the round was going to get started. But the bell never rang, and Chavez's cornermen were jawing with the referee about the ruling. I asked Lovato if he was surprised that the referee stopped the fight like that:

> **Lovato**: No, I wasn't surprised by the way the referee stopped the fight, it was kind of crazy 'cuz I didn't expect it to erupt into such a crazy happening.

Paul Chavez, who was working the corner for Anthony Chavez, grabbed the arm of the referee and pulled him in a pretty aggressive manner to demand an answer. That action would cost Mr. Chavez a few bucks later in the week.

While the cornermen and referee were arguing, Lovato walked over to a neutral corner and invited a fan who was yelling at him to "come on." That fan turned out to be former welterweight contender Henry Anaya Jr. He accepted Rudy's offer, climbed through the ropes, into the ring, and that's when all heck broke loose!

> **Anaya Jr.**: In the ring me and Rudy got into it. He called me out of the audience. Of course it turned into a street fight also. With fans getting involved. As you know boxing—it's a combat sport, and things like this are going to happen sometimes.

With people jumping into the ring and Anthony Chavez angry about being disqualified when he felt that it was Lovato who was breaking the rules, it turned into an actual battle royal.

I was seated right up against the ring and had a young man use my shoulder as a step-up into the ring. I was sitting next to fellow judge Walter Brown who was in a wheel chair. I tried to protect him from people climbing over us, since he was not mobile and would not be able to get away from it all. It was crazy, and it happened very fast. The cornermen were swatting at each other, and the referee was outnumbered as he stood defending himself in the middle of the mayhem.

The two boxers, trainers, security men, officials, and fans were all swinging, with blows being landed everywhere you looked. All that was missing was the 10-foot steel cage to make it a true main event. Lovato had fallen back and was hanging on to the ropes to keep from falling out of the ring. He was being held by a leather-jacketed security man with a baton in his right hand. The security man had his left arm around Lovato's torso when Anthony Chavez focused on his original opponent: he came at Lovato and threw a huge uppercut that knocked Rudy out of the grasp of the security man, out of the ring, and down to the floor.

I remember seeing one security man jump up into the ring, clad in black gloves with handcuffs hanging from his belt, facing off with a fan who had jumped into the fracas. The white-shirted fan threw a blazing bare-fisted five-punch combination that made the security guard turn and run back out of the ring. I later saw that same security guy come back into the ring from the other side after things had calmed down. He was obviously as impressed with the gentleman's hand speed as I was.

Things started to quiet down, and the promoter of the event began demanding that certain people be thrown out of the building by security.

Light-heavyweight Daniel "Pit Bull" Perez was fighting in the upcoming main event and told me:

> **Perez**: I was thinking—I've gotta put on a heck of a performance to beat *that* show!

Order was restored, and the next two fights (including the *real* main event) went off without further trouble.

> **Burke**: As bad as it got, it really was not *that* bad overall. We didn't have to cancel the following bouts, so that was good.

But that was not the end of the story for those involved in the riot. The New Mexico State Athletic Commission had me bring a little color television set and a VCR to their office, where they reviewed my VHS tape of the entire event before making a final assessment of the whole mess. When the smoke cleared, both boxers were fined $50 and were told their boxing licenses would be revoked until they paid up. Henry Anaya Sr. and Paul Chavez were also fined $50 for their part in the festivities. Rudy Lovato now looks back and laughs at the irony of how things have come full circle:

> **Lovato**: And now it's funny because I'm training Henry Jr.'s son, Henry Anaya III, and it's nice to have had the blessing of Mr. Henry Anaya—the godfather of New Mexico boxing—to train his grandson!

The video of the riot was shown, as part of an official's workshop, at the 1993 IBF convention in Albuquerque.

> **Burke**: We paid the referee an extra $50 for being involved in the best fight of the night!

Unfortunately, nobody paid to have the shoe print cleaned off of my nice shirt. I was going to show the entire event on my public access boxing show, but decided to leave that part out. I figured I'll just wait 24 years and write about it in a book...

A quarter of a century later, Lovato has been able to put the event in proper perspective:

> **Lovato**: I don't know if it's just me, but I sit back and look at my career and think about it, I am one of the original "OG Fighters" of New Mexico history. I've done it all—karate, kickboxing, boxing, jiu jitsu, trained professional fighters, and I kind of feel like Rocky Balboa—working in a restaurant.

CHAPTER FIVE

Real Talent

Alvin "Too Sweet" Hayes

November 18, 1986
Inglewood, California

Stroh's Beer was sponsoring a lightweight tournament that drew pro boxers from around the country to vie for the Stroh's title belt. On this night it was Missouri's Vernon "Yogi" Buchanan (16–4–1, 11 KO) matched up against Detroit's Alvin "Too Sweet" Hayes (27–2, 24 KO).

Both men had been seen by Los Angeles boxing fans in two previous fights each, and even though they weren't local, they were welcome additions to any fight card at the Forum.

The reason I include this fight, however, isn't because of the fight—it's because of the ring entrance of Alvin Hayes.

As Jimmy Lennon Sr. began to announce the match, and was introducing the dignitaries at ringside, Hayes came skipping down the aisle and climbed up into the ring. His opponent, Buchanan, was already in the ring and waiting for the fight to start. Hayes stood 6' 1" tall, but at only 135 lbs. he was quite a sight. Buchanan, at 5' 5" tall, was a more common height for the lightweight division.

Suddenly, the music changed and the bass line of Michael Jackson's *Billy Jean* began to play. Hayes froze, took off his robe, bit down on his bottom lip, and began to do a pretty good (and hilarious) imitation of Jackson. Spinning, lifting the leg and swinging it, he did everything but the moon walk. It was quite a spectacle that lasted for a good minute or so.

Ring announcer Jimmy Lennon caught a glimpse of the antics and had to stop his introductions as he tried to compose himself enough to continue. He could not. He lifted the microphone, started to talk into it, and just couldn't keep from laughing. Meanwhile, the "Alvin Hayes Show" continued. The music finally died down, Hayes returned to his corner, and Lennon was able to get on with the show.

Hayes probably should not have stopped dancing. He was dropped four times in the fight before finally being TKO'd in the sixth by Yogi Buchanan.

Hayes had some great talent ... and he boxed, too!

CHAPTER SIX

Just Like That?

Michael Dokes vs. Mike Weaver I

December 10, 1982
Las Vegas, Nevada

On this night, the WBA heavyweight championship of the world was at stake in a card held at Caesar's Palace, with both HBO and ABC on the scene to cover the event.

The defending champion, Mike "Hercules" Weaver, won the title with a miraculous one-punch knockout over undefeated champion John Tate in the 15th round. Tate was a member of the 1976 U.S. Olympic boxing team, winning the bronze medal; the undefeated WBA champion at 20–0; and a favorite in the match, but Weaver's knockout power left Tate face down in the middle of the ring with about two minutes left to go in the match. It was one of boxing's most memorable endings. Weaver had two successful title defenses of his belt, and was looking for a win over Michael Dokes to earn him a title unification rematch with WBC champ Larry Holmes. But now there was only one thing on his mind—defeat Michael Dokes.

Dokes was the unbeaten #1 WBA and WBC contender, and had plenty of amateur pedigree, at 24–0–1 with 14 wins by knockout. He was six years younger than the champion, only 24 years old, considered by many as the possible future of the heavyweight division at that time. The one blemish on his record was a 10-round draw against Ossie Ocasio in Puerto Rico. That draw was "avenged" as Dokes returned to Puerto Rico to knock out Ocasio in the first round of their rematch.

HBO carried the live broadcast of the heavyweight championship, and ABC had a team there to do a re-broadcast via tape delay, headlined by Keith Jackson. HBO had their "A team" on hand, with Barry Tompkins, Sugar Ray Leonard, Larry Merchant, and a very interested Larry Holmes working the show. The champion's inactivity seemed to be a concern for members of the broadcast team:

> **Merchant**: A lot of people who are in boxing think it's an excellent fight. And that whoever wins will be recognized by everyone as the 2nd best heavyweight in the world. Will *you* recognize them?
>
> **Holmes**: Yes, you have to kind of recognize whoever wins. The reason why they don't really recognize Mike Weaver is because he only fought twice in two years that he held the title. Mike Weaver is an inactive champion, and he should get out and fight more. And this could be a factor tonight. If he had demonstrated his boxing skills earlier, he might have been able to be the favorite coming into this fight.

Barry Tompkins and Sugar Ray Leonard also considered the layoff for Mike Weaver and if it could play into the fight:

> **Tompkins**: I think, Ray, the biggest question of this fight is Mike Weaver's ability to come back after having only really one fight in 25 months, a very difficult thing.
>
> **Leonard**: Well, as I always say, Barry, inactivity is a factor, always. But, with a guy like Mike Weaver, his physique, I mean this guy is physically strong. So, that could be a factor also against Michael Dokes.

As ring announcer Chuck Hull did the introductions, Dokes paced back and forth near his corner, looking like a vicious dog just waiting to be let off of the leash. Weaver was relaxed, looking confident and calm as he stood in his corner. He simply raised his arms and acknowledged the cheers of the crowd.

The two were brought to the center of the ring as they received the final instructions from referee Joey Curtis. Tompkins and Merchant remarked about Weaver's incredible build:

> **Tompkins**: There is the record of Mike Weaver. Nine losses, not indicative of his most recent performances,

sixteen knockouts, and a body that many people say his *hair* has muscles.

Merchant: He has muscles in places where other people don't have *places*!

Barry Tompkins mentioned that he was surprised at the fact that even though Weaver had that impressive muscular build, it was Dokes who was actually the bigger man. Taller and heavier.

The action instantly had the makings of a fight-of-the-year candidate as the challenger Dokes came right at Weaver letting his hands fly. The champion answered and caught Dokes with two solid left hands that stood him straight up for just a split-second.

Dokes continued to wade in and unleash bombs at the champion, catching him with a pair of left hands, the second sending Weaver to the canvas. The champion casually got up and walked over to the corner. He was up and waiting as the referee sent Dokes to the neutral corner. He waited calmly as the ref finished the mandatory 8-count.

The two were called back to action, and Dokes came racing across the ring at Weaver who laid on the ropes in a defensive posture. The champion was certainly hurt by the punch that put him on the floor, but he appeared steady, with solid legs under him, and seemed content to go into the defensive shell with hands high, and let Dokes burn himself out a bit.

Most of the punches thrown by Dokes were either missing or being blocked by the arms of Weaver. A left hook thrown by Weaver missed the target, and he continued to cover up as Dokes resumed the assault. Referee Joey Curtis stepped in to break the two—and it was this simple action that led to the end of the fight. Curtis pushed the two apart, turned to Dokes, grabbed him by the wrist, and raised his hand in victory. Weaver, who had stepped forward to continue the action off of what he thought was a break by the referee, suddenly realized what had been done.

The broadcasters were also shocked by the referee's actions:

Tompkins: And that's it. Just like that, this one is over!- Joey Curtis a little bit quick, I think, Ray.

Leonard: Well, Weaver still had his senses, I mean, he still was up. He was hit by a lot of good shots.

Tompkins: It took one minute and three seconds.

They weren't the only ones in disbelief. On the ABC tape delay broadcast, Keith Jackson did not know what to make of the stoppage as it happened before his eyes:

Jackson: And the fight has been STOPPED! Joey Curtis, the referee, has stopped the fight in the very first round. Weaver, leaning back on the ropes, is in a posture of utter disgust. He did not obviously feel, nor did his corner people feel, that he was in any danger after being knocked down. It could be that everybody is so sensitive after the Deuk Kim tragedy. The fight was stopped, suddenly, by Joey Curtis. 1:03 of the first round. Mike Weaver standing in utter disbelief.

As Weaver turned to his corner, and then walked a few steps in that direction, the look in his eyes was one of total disbelief. A pained half smile of incredulity. Dokes jumped a few times, and then fell on his back with the realization that he was suddenly the WBA heavyweight world champion.

As Dokes got to his feet and made his way through the crowded ring toward Weaver's corner, things became heated between members of the two camps. There was a scuffle with lots of pushing and shoving, but it was stopped just short of a full-fledged riot by a quick acting Caesars Palace security team.

Just as the melee in the ring began to settle down, the fans began chanting their displeasure at the way the bout was stopped. A chant of "Bulls**t! Bulls**t!" filled the air of the packed Caesars Palace sports pavilion:

Tompkins: And the crowd is saying it all!

Tompkins asked WBC heavyweight champion Larry Holmes what he thought of the stoppage. Holmes' microphone remarks were not totally audible, though it was clear that he did not agree with the referee's decision. Tompkins continued:

Tompkins: Well, it was a very strange ending, and we will get an opportunity to see this. The crowd not liking it at all, I have to be honest, I don't blame them.

Leonard: I have to re-evaluate on Larry Holmes here. Weaver's been in some big, some heavy brawls. He's been hit, he's been hurt, and he always has a tendency to come back. This fight was stopped, I felt soon, *too* soon!

Tompkins: I don't think there's any question about that.

Dokes and Weaver hugged each other and just shook their heads as they talked. A few scuffles continued to break out around them, but it seemed the two fighters were not blaming each other for what happened.

Referee Joey Curtis was questioned about the stoppage:

Merchant: Barry, I'm here with Mr. Curtis, the referee who stopped the fight. Why did you stop the fight?

Curtis: I stopped the fight because he was taking several punches to the head and to the body. When I stepped in there after the knockdown, I asked him if he was alright. He didn't answer me correctly, but I still let the fight go a little bit more. He continually stood to take punches to the head and to the body. I figured that he'd had enough and I stopped the fight.

Merchant: You have a reputation of allowing fights to go on. Has the recent furor over the death of the Korean fighter right here, in Caesar's Palace, had any influence on you stopping this fight?

Curtis: That didn't make my decision at all. Like I said before, he was taking several punches to the head, and several punches to the body. When I gave him the count, I didn't like the way he answered me. That's why I let him go a little further, and that's why I stopped him the second time.

Merchant: In the eyes of a ringsider, even though he wasn't returning fire, he still seemed to have his faculties.

Curtis: Not to me, when I gave him the count. He didn't look like he had the count after the, after the 8-count.

Again Tompkins asked Larry Holmes what he thought about the explanation. Holmes' microphone was still muted, but he could be heard voicing his displeasure with the answer given by referee Curtis.

On the ABC broadcast, Keith Jackson grilled the referee:

Jackson: We are with the man who is bound to be at the center of this post-fight tempest, the referee Joey Curtis. Joey, why did you stop it?

Curtis: After he went down in the first knockdown, I gave him the count of 8. I looked into his eyes. He responded just a little bit, not the way I really wanted, but I figured I'd give him another chance. And the second time, he was taking very, very bad punches to the head, and to the body, and that's when I decided, I wasn't going to have another Deuk-Koo Kim on my hands.

Jackson: So you felt the man was, in effect, defenseless.

Curtis: Yes, he was. Yes, he was. I thought it was a very, very good fight right up to that time, but he kept on punching at him. And when [Weaver] couldn't respond to me after the first knockdown, that's why again, I let him continue a little longer. And, when I saw he was taking more punches, I thought I would stop it.

Jackson then asked Mike Weaver about the stoppage:

Jackson: Now, Mike Weaver, his side of it. You appeared enraged when it was called, Michael. Were you hurt?

Weaver: No, I was not hurt. Dokes caught me with a good left hook, and naturally, it dropped me down, but I got up immediately. I wasn't hurt. I really don't know why the referee stopped the fight, I really don't. I mean, I was not hurt a bit. I really don't know why they did it.

Jackson: He says that you did not respond as much as he would have wanted you to after the knockdown.

Weaver: Well, how much did he want me to respond? He hit me with a good left hook. He knocked me down, and uh, what else could I do? I mean, I was throwing punches. I mean, it's nothing but a set-up.

Weaver's chief trainer, Don Manuel, seemed to agree:

Manuel: This is the championship of the world. I know that they are having lots of controversy. And I feel like I know when a fight should be stopped. I would have stopped it myself if I thought he had been in trouble. I always have. But he wasn't in that kind of trouble. They should have let the fight continue. And I'm definitely going to, I've already protested it. I want a hearing on it right away. Before Dokes fights anybody else, I want a hearing on this.

ABC's Jackson was not finished trying to make some sense of the quick stoppage. He next talked with the new champion, Michael Dokes:

Dokes: He was taking blows. He didn't offer no type of offense. So it wasn't up to me. I'm just the fighter.

Jackson: Michael, I've known you since you were a teenager in the amateur boxing, and you always did like to start fast. I have never seen you start faster than you did in this fight.

Dokes: That's one of my greatest attributes, my speed, along with developing and concentrating on my power at this point. So, you know, to me, I seen that he was cold, he wasn't sweltering, at all. He didn't look like he was lively or frisky at this point, so I thought I'd jump right on him.

Jackson then deposed Harold Buck, the chief inspector for the Nevada State Athletic Commission:

Jackson: Your comment on the stoppage of the fight?

Buck: Keith, the only thing that I would have to say is that, sitting at ringside you don't have as good a view of the fight as the referee. And at his discretion, he can make the decision to stop the fight, feeling that a fighter is in trouble.

Jackson finished his line of interrogations with the ring physician, Dr. Donald Romeo, who was pretty clear on where he stood on the matter:

Jackson: Now a word with the ring physician assigned by the Nevada State Athletic Commission, and a man who has seen, goodness knows, how many fights, championship as well as otherwise. Dr. Donald Romeo. Your reaction?

Romeo: My reaction is—the fight was stopped too soon.

Jackson: You had no access to the fighter, did you? You did not take a look at him?

Romeo: I did not.

Jackson: Should you have been called for a consultation?

Romeo: I would have certainly thought that would have been the proper thing to do.

Jackson: From your position on that side of the ring, where Mike Weaver went down, did he appear hurt to you?

Romeo: He did not.

Jackson: The referee said that he took four hard right hands to the head, and that's why he stepped in.

Romeo: Those I saw. But if you have seen Mike Weaver fight before, you will know that he is a very slow starter, Keith. I have seen him personally take quite a few punches. [He knocked out Gerrie] Coetzee with one punch three rounds later, after taking nine rounds of a pretty good pummeling. I have seen him ... and you saw him, too... I saw this on television, in Knoxville where Tate had the fight won, 15th round, one punch, Mike took him out. Mike is a slow starter, and, I definitely think the fight was stopped too soon. Now, I must admit... Of course, with all of the controversy which has happened in the fight game, I can give the referee a plus on that. But by the same token, this was a championship fight. And I just feel it was stopped too soon.

It was an unsatisfying way for Michael Dokes to win his first world title, and a terrible way for Mike Weaver to lose it. After a protest was filed, Weaver was given an immediate rematch with Dokes. About five months later they did it "for real," with the bout ending in a majority decision draw. Dokes retained his title, but Weaver proved to the world that the result of the first fight was a fluke.

Dokes lost his title to Gerrie Coetzee in his next fight. He would be involved in many more heavyweight bouts, but most boxing pundits feel that even though he did bring lots of excitement to the game, his full potential was never realized. He retired in 1997.

Weaver went on to be involved in many more high-level heavyweight bouts, including one more shot at a major heavyweight title against Pinklon Thomas for his WBC world championship. Weaver ended his pro career in 2000 with a rematch against Larry Holmes. He was a huge player in a very competitive heavyweight era.

CHAPTER SEVEN

Butt Out!

Donald Curry vs. Tony Montgomery

February 7, 1987
Las Vegas, Nevada

One of boxing's top stars—Donald "The Lone Star Cobra" Curry (25–1, 20 KO)—was coming off of his first loss, in a bout with Lloyd Honeyghan. He lost his unified welterweight title belts in the process. Curry was looking to assure the boxing world that he would be back for those belts.

His opponent was a promising young unbeaten fighter out of Detroit, Michigan, named Tony Montgomery. Montgomery was 17–0 winning 10 by knockout, and he had stopped 7 of his last 9 opponents. His record was impressive, but there were few recognizable names among those wins. Boxing historian (and CompuBox punch counter) Lee Groves was tuned in:

> **Groves**: A little more than four months before this fight Curry was on top of the world. He was the undisputed welterweight champion and on a path that could lead him to a 154-pound title, then a culminating fight with undisputed middleweight champion Marvelous Marvin Hagler, the number-one pound-for-pound fighter in the world.

The bout was set for 12 rounds, with the vacant USBA junior middleweight championship up for grabs. CBS televised the contest, with Tim Brant and Gil Clancy at ringside doing the commentary, and setting the table:

> **Brant**: Certainly the most interesting aspect of this fight are all the questions that have been surrounding Donald Curry. This is his first fight since he lost the undisputed world welterweight title, that was against

Lloyd Honeyghan in September. And now he comes into this fight, Gil, with an awful lot of questions.

Clancy: Well, Tim, in that fight he said he had managerial problems, he had trouble making the weight. The managerial problems are behind him, he's coming in at a comfortable hundred and fifty-four, he certainly did look strong in the gym. However, he took a pretty good beating in the Honeyghan fight. It's going to be interesting to see how he reacts when he gets hit.

Both fighters looked serious and focused as referee James Molinell gave them the pre-fight instructions. They tapped gloves without incident.

They both came out looking a little tight to start round 1, Montgomery was using his feet to glide around the ring while Curry went right to work using his patient, stand-up counter-punching style. It was a close round with both fighters having their moments. Curry's edge in power was evident as his punches were fewer, but served up with accuracy and impact.

Groves: Montgomery was one of Curry's sparring partners for the Honeyghan fight, so the ex-champ knew, at least generally, the type of fighter he was facing. But he couldn't have known how Montgomery would react in the heat of real combat as opposed to a controlled sparring situation. Had he known, he might have thought twice about picking him as his comeback opponent.

Curry started the second round with a dedication to throwing a left hand to the body. Montgomery lunged forward with his head, and earned a quick warning from referee Molinell.

Clancy: Montgomery really used his head. Curry's supposed to be the veteran, Montgomery came in like a billy goat. The referee warned him, and properly so.

A little more than halfway through the round, Montgomery did it again, launching the top of his head at Curry.

Clancy: Oh, and there goes that billy goat again!

Montgomery began to move less, instead standing in with Curry. Not a good tactical decision. With 14 seconds left in the round, Curry caught him in an exchange, with a right hand that put Montgomery to the deck. He got up looking a little unsteady, but the bell immediately rang following the mandatory 8-count to end the round.

> **Groves**: A right cross stunned Montgomery late in the first round and following an exchange in round two Montgomery leaned in with the top of his head and struck Curry with the first of what would be numerous head butts. The weakening process unfolded with stunning speed and the effects on Montgomery's body and mind were evident. A flush one-two to the chin sent Montgomery down in the waning moments of round 2, the first time he was floored either as a pro or an amateur. It must have been a shock to Montgomery's system, and the way he dealt with that shock would prove memorable … and outrageous.

Donald Curry came out for round 3 looking confident, patiently walking his opponent down:

> **Clancy**: Montgomery's never been on the deck before, amateur or pro. That was a new experience for him. Let's see how he reacts.
>
> **Brant**: Now he's on his bicycle, trying to stay away from Donald Curry.

Montgomery was not running away, but obviously needed to find a way to avoid getting caught again while scoring. Late in the round, Curry landed another hard right hand that seemed to hurt Montgomery. With fifteen seconds left in the round, Montgomery snuck a head butt in on Curry, and then followed it with an obvious battering-ram style head butt that caused the referee to halt the action and give him a clear warning, pointing his finger to his face and telling him: "Watch that head! Watch that head!"

> **Clancy**: Oh, there goes that head again. That's three times now.
>
> **Brant**: And he's warned.
>
> **Clancy**: That's actually helping Montgomery now, because the clock is winding down.

After being warned, with just two seconds left in the round, Montgomery pushed Curry back with the top of his head again just before the bell sounded:

> **Clancy**: There he goes again with the head!

Round 4 began, and it was not long until Montgomery snuck in another short butt to Curry's chin, and then followed it up with another obvious lunging head butt. Referee James Molinell's patience had been tested for the last time. He stopped the clock and deducted one point from Montgomery for his actions. Montgomery seemed to accept it, not complaining or pleading at all.

The action resumed, and Curry continued his control of the bout. With elbows in tight, Curry blocked the body shots attempted by Montgomery. Montgomery again jumped in with his head, but it didn't connect. The referee just reminded him to "watch that head." Montgomery then shot a weak left hand and was countered with a rock hard left hand by Curry that made him back away looking just a bit shaky.

> **Brant**: Left hook has Montgomery backing off. He looks a little bit dazed.
>
> **Clancy**: He was hurt by that punch.
>
> **Brant**: Curry coming in now, trying to finish him off.
>
> **Clancy**: He's going to have to offer some resistance, and they're not going to be far from stopping this fight.
>
> **Brant**: Curry is just measuring him now.
>
> **Clancy**: The only resistance he offers is with that head butt. Punches, he's not using.

As the action continued, Curry stalked his opponent and landed a beautiful left hand to the body that froze Montgomery for a split second, and then as he stepped back Curry landed a hard uppercut that sent him to the deck for the second time in the fight. It was a beautiful compact right uppercut that snapped Montgomery's head, and then as Curry stepped back, he crashed forward, his fall helping him avoid a short left hook that Curry fired. Montgomery was alert and remained squatting as he listened to the referee's count, standing up as it reached eight. The ref seemed concerned about the condition of

Montgomery and asked him several times whether he wanted to continue. Montgomery nodded that he did.

The ref waved the two back to action, and Montgomery seemed to be trying to convince himself that he was not hurt, but as he fired a right hand that missed, and then barked something at Curry shaking his head, Curry caught him with a short right-uppercut / short left-hook combination that sent Montgomery down for a third time in the fight.

He again waited, this time on one knee, and listened to the referee's count, standing up at the count of nine. The bell sounded just as the referee called for action to continue. Montgomery walked back to his corner looking like a beaten man.

Between rounds 4 and 5, the ring doctor checked Montgomery's condition. He was game and came out for round 5.

Montgomery started the fifth round working, and showed signs of life, landing a nice right uppercut of his own. That success was short-lived as Curry began to land solid shots. With about two minutes left in the round, Curry had Montgomery in retreat again as he continued his methodical but relentless attack. It seemed as if Montgomery felt the only way to keep Curry off of him was by using his head. He again ducked his head and lunged forward at the aggressive Curry.

> **Groves**: It was clear that Montgomery was unraveling ... not only was he being outclassed, he was getting tired. And he had eight long rounds to go. The fifth round was no better for Montgomery and Curry appeared on his way to a clinical stoppage victory. His blows struck with soul-sapping power and Montgomery knew as well as anyone that his time in the ring was nearing an end.

After several attempted butts, the referee called for a stoppage and deducted another point from Montgomery. The action resumed and as the two came into close contact, Montgomery pushed forward with his head.

> **Clancy**: I think Montgomery is looking to get disqualified. That's the only thing I can think of.

As Curry worked Montgomery over in surgical fashion with an assortment of sharp, precise punches, Montgomery jumped at Curry with his head, catching him flush in the face with a hard head butt that made Curry grimace and step away.

> **Groves**: The worst thing that a fighter could have on his record is a "KO by" designation because that is proof of another man's superiority over him. Montgomery didn't want that to be his first blemish and so he shifted into survival mode. Part of that survival mode was to butt Curry ... and keep butting him. It not only slowed Curry's assault, it also was the only way Montgomery could inflict visible pain.

Referee James Molinell had seen enough. He put his arm around Montgomery and waived the fight to a stop.

> **Groves**: When Montgomery connected with the hardest butt of the fight—a butt that made Curry wince and turn away—the Ref had no choice but to stop the fight and disqualify Montgomery. Yes, he lost, but the ledger would read "L DQ" instead of "KO by."

It was a disqualification at 2:29 of round 5, a win for "The Lone Star Cobra" Donald Curry.

> **Clancy**: And he did exactly as I said. He looked to get disqualified, he got disqualified.

Curry was angered by the conduct of his opponent, and as the referee was walking Montgomery back to his corner, with one hand on his shoulder and the other hand in the air signaling that the fight was over, Curry calmly walked up to Montgomery and fired a right hand over the referee's shoulder, connecting on the left ear of Montgomery.

> **Groves**: For the second straight fight, butts figured into the result of his fight and he wanted to send a message not only to Montgomery but to anyone else who would think of using butts to stop him. He walked across the ring and threw a right hand over the referee's shoulder. Soon a legion of angry people began flooding the ring and a riot appeared imminent.

It wasn't a "knockout" punch, but it was a good stiff poke. He then turned around and calmly walked back to his corner.

> **Brant**: Oh, and Donald Curry comes up and throws

a punch at Montgomery's head after the fight had ended. They're throwing things in the ring! Oh, it's ugly, Gil.

Things immediately started to heat up, with fans throwing objects into the ring and angry cornermen stepping into the ring. Montgomery's trainer, Sunny Ray, was furious.

Clancy: Yes, it certainly is. Sunny Ray, an ex-fighter himself and a pretty good one, wants to go over and fight with the Donald Curry people.

Brant: Sunny Ray, pushing security people, there he is. Unsportsmanlike, and the game of boxing does not need that right now.

It was a wild scene as Caesar's Palace security people in yellow shirts immediately jumped up onto the ring apron and lined the ring to prevent outsiders from joining the action. State athletic commission officials in suits and uniformed police officers were trying to keep the peace. They did a good job.

Order was restored pretty quickly, but emotions were running hot. Curry's side was mad at Montgomery for all of the head butts, and Montgomery's side was angry about the free shot after the fight was stopped.

Clancy: Well, that was quite an exciting ending.

Brant: There's no place in boxing for that. Donald Curry is an outstanding champion.

Clancy: Now, I imagine it will be up to the commission to say whether they want to fine Tony Montgomery? Hold up his purse? Something's gonna have to happen.

After things settled down, CBS's Tim Brant talked to Curry about the fight:

Brant: I'm standing here with Donald Curry, the new United States Boxing Association junior middleweight [champion]. And the first thing I'm going to ask you, Donald, is about the punch after the fight was stopped.

Curry: Well, he kept using his head, trying the head buttin'. I went on with it for a while. I just got tired of it.

Brant: You knew the fight had ended?

Curry: Well, I knew the fight was about over. I think when I dropped him with the right hand, that's when I hurt my right hand, I couldn't use my right hand and I started throwing one punches, and tryin' to get him out of there with one punch.

Brant: The head butts, he kept coming at you with the head butt. Were you conscious of the fact, of what Honeyghan did to you?

Curry: Yeah, not really that. I was just worried about getting cut. I was in control of the head butts. I wasn't too much worried; it was just kind of aggravating me that he kept doing it. I know he was desperate, he was losing, wasn't nothing he could do, but y'know, you don't do that in the ring. That's bad sportsmanship.

Brant and Curry then watched the slow motion replay of what happened, and Curry explained how he saw it:

Brant: Alright, now that was the last head butt, that's when they stopped the fight. You walked away.

Curry: Yeah, he butted me in the nose and it hurt. And I think that's what upset me the most.

Brant: And there's the punch afterwards.

Curry: I had to get him back for one of those head butts.

Tony Montgomery was then brought over to talk to Tim Brant about what had just happened. The former Donald Curry sparring partner gave his side of the story:

Brant: Your reaction to the punch after the fight was stopped?

Montgomery: Well, he was, that was out of, madness. He was mad because I was buttin' him. You know, hey, I don't know. It was, y'know, it was a shot after the bell, what can I say? I'm not upset about it or anything like that, but I'll be back, y'know. That's just my first loss. And he was the better man today; I have nothing else to say. He was the better man ... today.

The Nevada State Athletic Commission held up the purses of both fighters until a review of the entire event was made.

The next year Donald Curry added the WBC Jr. middleweight title belt to his collection. He would fight another 10 years and be involved in a few more world title challenges. It was not the last time that Curry would have problems being butted by opponents.

> **Groves**: Of course, that didn't stop Carlos Santos (Curry's next fight) from using his head to combat Curry. He, too, was disqualified in round five for excessive butting.

Tony Montgomery won the vacant Michigan junior middleweight title in his next fight. He fought on for about 5 years after the bout with Donald Curry.

CHAPTER EIGHT

Sudden Disappointment

Nate Campbell vs. Isaac Hlatshwayo

April 7, 2006
Tampa, Florida

An ESPN2 televised event at the Florida State Fairgrounds Hall featured South Africa's undefeated Isaac "The Angel" Hlatshwayo putting his IBO lightweight title on the line against hard-punching contender Nate "The Galaxy Warrior" Campbell. The bout was also named as a title eliminator for the more prestigious IBF #2 ranking.

Hlatshwayo won the IBO title nine months earlier, in South Africa, where he defended it successfully several months later. This would be his second defense, and a big chance for him to be seen on national television. Campbell was the former North American Boxing Federation junior lightweight champion, with a reputation as a knockout artist. It was an excellent matchup.

Campbell started well, landing hard body shots, and looking more seasoned with his experience showing in little moves that helped him score and slip the return shots. Hlatshwayo looked to be naturally bigger as they were working in close.

As the bell sounded to end round 2, Hlatshwayo stuck Campbell with a little poke, and Campbell answered with a pretty good left hand thrown over the shoulder of referee Frank Santore Jr. who admonished both of them for going after the bell. It was an important fight to both combatants, and emotions were running high.

The fight continued in much the same pattern. Campbell was more elusive, more fluid in his movement, much more versatile in his boxing style. Hlatshwayo was able to move forward, and even though he was robotic in his movement, it gave the impression of control to the judges.

Campbell's versatility may have turned from an asset to a liability as he was content to move and be tricky, but this allowed Hlatshwayo to adopt a much more aggressive stance.

After eight rounds, ESPN2's Teddy Atlas' unofficial scorecard showed Hlatshwayo pulling ahead by one point after giving Campbell the first three rounds.

Between rounds 9 and 10, Campbell's trainer, Lenny Perez, was heard telling his man, "You just lost the last three rounds ... can you beat this guy?"

The final three rounds were close. Campbell looked like the fighter with the pressure of finishing strong on his shoulders after falling behind in the middle rounds.

It looked like a close decision was brewing. Teddy Atlas had the fight scored 115–114 for Isaac Hlathswayo on his unofficial scorecard for the consideration of the broadcast viewers.

While the scorecards were being tabulated by the commission, the two fighters looked concerned, and they hugged each other as they awaited the announcement of the decision. It was an important step in the career of both boxers, with Campbell hoping that a win would catapult him into a big-money title fight, and Hlatshwayo looking to remain unbeaten and move up into title consideration with a major win on his record.

With ring announcer M. Mark Biero giving the signal that he was ready to make the announcement, ESPN2's Joe Tessitore asked:

> **Tessitore**: Waiting for the decision to be tabulated here in Tampa. Isaac Hlathswayo is *Ring* magazine's #8 lightweight. A perfect 24–0. His brother died last year. He overcame that tragedy, used it as an inspiration, and he made his brother a promise that he would stay perfect and undefeated and retire that way. Nate Campbell on the other side, a contending lightweight after being a former world-title challenger at junior lightweight. All the momentum with the win over Kid Diamond, but which way will it go? Did Isaac Hlatshwayo do it and stay perfect? Let's find out with M. Mark Biero.

The ring announcer began reading the scorecards as the ESPN2 broadcast showed a split screen with the two hopefuls looking very concerned, concentrating on every word that was announced to the world:

> **Biero**: Ladies and gentlemen, we have a split decision. Judge Mark Streisand scores the bout 115–113, Campbell. Judge Rich Green sees it 116–112, Hlatshwayo. And judge Peter Trematerra scores the bout 117–111 to the winner, by split decision of the IBF eliminator and new…

With the words "and new" challenger Nate Campbell fell to the ground with happiness as he believed he had just taken a huge step forward in his boxing career. Hlatshwayo looked around with a confused expression, taking a few steps across the ring in a daze. Meanwhile, the ring announcer was finishing up the announcement that was not picked up by the two boxers:

> **Biero**: IBO lightweight champion—Isaac Hlatshwayo, Hlatshwayo.

Campbell was nearly in tears as he accepted congratulatory hugs from his team members. The fans, though, picked up the full announcement and showered the ring with booing and jeers as they were aware that their hometown fighter had failed to gain the IBO title. The two fighters continued to express their misled emotions.

> **Tessitore**: Isaac Hlatshwayo doesn't understand that he just won, because Nate Campbell is celebrating in the ring. Nate Campbell thinks that he won … he didn't win. He lost, and there's no way a 117–111 would be for Campbell!

As Campbell broke away from the hugs and celebration, he turned to see the referee shaking his head "no" and raising the hand of Hlatshwayo. Campbell froze, realizing with a look of total disbelief that he had instantly gone from winner to loser. A sense of shock seemed to overtake him. Many around him still did not realize what was happening as a woman came up to him with a big smile on her face, kissed him on the shoulder, and offered congratulations as he told her that he didn't win. You could feel the sense of confusion as she said, "What?" and then turned to the referee asking, "Who won?"

Campbell wandered around the ring continuing to hear congratulations from others inside the ring who did not realize that he had just lost a split decision.

> **Tessitore**: He's finding out right now that he lost!
>
> **Atlas**: And now, he's [Hlatshwayo] thrilled, and he is obviously surprised and pleasantly surprised. The language barrier playing into that effect right there.
>
> **Tessitore**: Unbelievable. Nate Campbell heard "and new"—that's because Isaac Hlatshwayo has the title, so he just assumed he won that title, but he didn't. Hlatshwayo won the split decision. And you knew it when 117–111 was announced.
>
> **Atlas**: Campbell going down on his knees hearing "new" and thinking he won. Hlatshwayo, not speaking the English language, seeing the reaction of Campbell, thinking, "Gee, I lost." And then all of a sudden being told, "No, you won!"
>
> **Tessitore**: You know, I say it all the time. You never know what you are going to get with this sport. And it never stops surprising you. That's a new one right there. Nate Campbell thought he won, he lost. The split-decision win. Isaac Hlatshwayo remains undefeated 25–0.

Campbell handled it all in a very dignified way. He did not make a scene, he listened as Hlatshwayo came to him and told him something in his ear. You couldn't blame him much if he had erupted with anger after the 180-degree turn in emotions with the realization of what had just happened. As the broadcast signed off, Hlatshwayo was standing proudly with the IBO title belt over his shoulder and his hand being raised again by the referee just to make sure that everyone in the venue knew that he was the official winner of this bout.

Hlatshwayo would fight for seven more years and win the IBO and IBF welterweight titles.

Campbell's standing in the game was not hurt in the least by this close loss. He fought on and earned the IBF, WBA, and WBO lightweight world titles before calling it a career in 2014.

CHAPTER NINE

A Heavenly Sign

Johnny Tapia

May 27, 2012

As my wife and I got ready for church, I opened the drawer that held some of my older t-shirts, and saw one with my friend, former world champion Johnny Tapia, on it. It was a shirt that featured the poster from Johnny's 1996 fight with Hugo Soto on the front. Johnny was dressed in black, standing with his WBO super flyweight title belt around his waist, with the lights of Albuquerque behind him. I forgot I even had that shirt, and had not worn it in over a decade and a half. I decided to wear it to church that morning, and wore it the rest of the day.

My wife noticed the shirt and said, "Where did you get that shirt from?" I told her, "I've had it for years, just never wore it. I don't know why, but I felt like going through that drawer with the old t-shirts and I wanted to wear it today."

That evening, the phone rang. It was my mother calling me from Albuquerque to inform me that Johnny had passed away. I didn't really believe it at first. I thought, *Mom is probably just confused about what she heard*, so I checked with some friends. It was true. At age 45, Johnny was gone.

I went in to tell my wife what had happened and she just pointed at my shirt. I looked down and it struck me in an eerie moment. We looked at each other for a few seconds and I walked away in a little bit of a daze. My friend was gone, a man who had thrilled millions of fight fans around the world, battled demons, and cheated death for all of those years. Why? Why, of all the days, all the months, all those years, did I go to that drawer and pull out that shirt?

I take it as a sign from the Lord, his mysterious way of telling my wife and I that it is OK, that "Johnny is with me now. You will see him again." I believe that, and look forward to telling Johnny about what happened, in person, when I see him next.

CHAPTER TEN

No One Was Safe

Willie DeWitt vs. Pedro Cardenas

June 1982
Las Vegas, Nevada

The North American Amateur Boxing Championships drew teams from the US, Cuba, Mexico, Canada, Puerto Rico, and the Dominican Republic, all vying for the medals being awarded during the tournament.

The heavyweight fight between Cuba's Pedro Cardenas and Willie DeWitt of Canada would become infamous. Yes, this was an *amateur* bout, but it deserves mention here. It was just that crazy.

The bout started fast with the two fighters coming straight at each other and trading blows. Just seconds in, the heavy-handed DeWitt landed a right that froze the Cuban fighter, and followed that with a left that turned Cardenas' head, causing referee Bert Lowes to step in and administer a standing 8-count to the Cuban. After giving the full 8-count, Lowes made the motion to Cardenas as if to say, "Keep your guard up." He should have listened to his own advice.

The action continued for just a few seconds before Lowes felt that Cardenas was still not fully in control of his faculties, and stepped in to administer a second standing 8-count. In amateur boxing, any combination of three knockdowns and/or standing 8-counts in a round results in a technical knockout (RSC—Referee Stops Contest). Cardenas did not complain as he was being counted. At the end of the count, an anxious DeWitt began to step in, but was told to step back before the referee would allow the assault to continue.

DeWitt charged in and landed wicked shots that looked like it was the end for the Cuban fighter. But, as referee Lowes stepped in seemingly to call a halt to the bout and rescue the stunned boxer, Cardenas launched a left hand that unintentionally caught the 62-year-old referee right on the chin.

Lowes froze instantly and fell face first, with his hands at his sides, bouncing off of the second from the bottom rope, right at the chest area. The two boxers stepped aside and looked at each other with total bewilderment on their faces.

The referee rolled over onto his back and semi-sat up with a blank look on his face. The attending ring physician hurried over to check on the stunned Lowes, who seemed to be more embarrassed than injured. The doctor took out his pen-light to look into the eyes of the referee as the confused Lowes opened his mouth while the doctor checked the pupils of his eyes.

Lowes insisted he was OK, and could continue, but the officials decided that a new referee should be brought in to finish the bout. Lowes, who suffered a cut to the bridge of his nose from the fall into the ropes, took a seat at ringside while Ulises Rodrigues of Venezuela was called to duty, stepping in and picking up the action where it had left off. Rodrigues was a much smaller man than Bert Lowes, but the officials felt he could handle himself with the two brutes in the ring.

A jury of officials were consulted as to where the bout stood. They concluded that the third standing 8-count had not been officially administered by Lowes, so the bout could continue with two standing 8-counts being assigned to the Cuban fighter. One more in the round would mean the end of the bout and a win for DeWitt.

As the bell sounded and the bout continued, the two went straight at each other, and the Cuban landed a solid left hook that dropped DeWitt on the seat of his trunks. Just seconds into the continuation of the bout, DeWitt got to his feet quickly, but had to take the full standing 8-count from the new referee.

The wild action continued as the two sluggers traded blows. DeWitt was caught with another bomb that staggered him, and caused Rodrigues to administer a second standing 8-count to the wobbly Canadian fighter.

Immediately after the count, Cardenas jumped at DeWitt with a wild swing that missed and caused *him* to fall to the canvas from his own desperate momentum. It wasn't a knockdown, so the referee made a motion for Cardenas to wipe his gloves, which was ignored as the command to "box" was given.

The two were clinching as the tiny referee commanded them to break and tried to push Cardenas back. Rodrigues was struggling as the two heavyweights, knowing they were just one knockdown or standing 8-count away from victory, were furiously trying to deliver their finishing shot.

With six seconds left in this wild opening round, Cardenas dipped his head and spun around. It had to be tempting for DeWitt to fire at the open target, but he showed some restraint and held back. The referee stopped the bout to give Cardenas a warning. The round finished up the last few seconds and both fighters went back to their corners having survived one of the wildest rounds ever witnessed in boxing, amateur or pro. The crowd rose to their feet in unison, hands raised in the air, in total appreciation of the hearts shown by the two fighters, and the wild events they just witnessed.

Round 2 picked up right where the first round left off. Referee Rodrigues had a heck of a time convincing Cardenas to step back after breaking the clinches of the two fighters.

About one minute into the round, Rodrigues stepped in to break the two and got tagged by a left hand that grazed both DeWitt's chin and the side of referee Rodrigues' head. The referee was not hurt, and the action continued. The crowd was howling with excitement.

Seconds later, the referee stepped in to break the two fighters when Cardenas launched a left hand during the break that caught DeWitt square on the jaw. DeWitt was not staggered, but the referee stopped the action to give a stern warning to the Cuban not to hit on the break again.

Cardenas did it once more. It looked like the referee was going to deduct points from the Cuban boxer, but instead, he took Cardenas over to the corner so that the ring doctor could look at a cut that had developed over the fighter's eye.

After the doctor had examined Cardenas and found no reason to stop the fight, the action continued as the two locked up like pit bulls. DeWitt, with blood coming from his mouth, landed a huge right hand, followed with a combination to the body and head. Cardenas crumpled to the canvas. He rose up with blood running down his forehead, looking wobbly and hurt. Rodrigues had seen enough and waved the bout to a stop.

This was an incredible bout that saw both fighters dropped twice, standing 8-counts, a referee who was KO'd, a backup referee nearly KO'd, warnings, and blood.

You may remember seeing a referee getting KO'd during the opening of the television show *Malcolm in the Middle*—this was it! And now you know the story behind that incredible scene.

CHAPTER ELEVEN

Who Stopped It?

Kelly Pavlik vs. Fulgencio Zuniga

October 7, 2005
Las Vegas, Nevada

The Aladdin Hotel & Casino was the site for Kelly "The Ghost" Pavlik, from Youngstown, Ohio, to take on Colombia's Fulgencio Zuniga for the vacant North American Boxing Federation middleweight championship.

The bout was originally scheduled as a semi-main event for the Christy Martin vs Lucia Rijker fight on July 30 at Mandalay Bay, also in Las Vegas. When Rijker suffered a torn Achilles tendon in training, that bout was scrubbed, and with it the entire card was cancelled.

Pavlik's co-manager, Cameron Dunkin, was able to land this fight as the main event on the Aladdin Hotel show on the Spanish-language Telefutura network. It was a bout that was just too good not to happen. Boxing video collector Carlo Pineda (no relation to Zuniga's trainer Orlando Pineda) recalls his thinking going into the bout:

> **Pineda**: Kelly "The Ghost" Pavlik vs. Fulgencio Zuniga was on the same weekend as the scheduled José Luis Castillo vs. Diego "Chico" Corrales title match, which was the fight getting the most exposure in Las Vegas that weekend. Going into this fight there was interest in seeing just how good Pavlik was, as he was taking a big step up in competition. Zuniga was a very good fighter from Colombia who could turn out to be a good test for the rising star. It often seems Latin American, especially Colombian, fighters we haven't heard from before have

made a name for themselves in the USA after conquering their favored American opponent on foreign soil to win their title. Mauricio Pastrana defeated boxing great Michael Carbajal, and Ener Julio edged Randall Bailey. Both bouts took place in Las Vegas.

Zuniga was 17–1–1, with 16 by knockout. He was the IBA middleweight champion, but that title was not on the line. Instead, he sought to add the NABF middleweight title to his collection. His only loss came against Daniel Santos in a bid for the WBO junior middleweight championship two years earlier. His punching power was proven, and his credentials as a contender were solid.

Kelly Pavlik was undefeated at 26–0 with 23 knockouts. He was a fast-rising contender who felt ready to claim his first title belt.

Pineda: Kelly Pavlik always reminded me of Diego Corrales. He had the height and reach over most of his opponents, yet didn't mind fighting on the inside, as he was very effective at throwing hard, fast combinations at close quarters. This often spells for explosive, entertaining battles.

Pavlik was ready to showcase his aggressive style to the Latino boxing fans that would be tuned in on Telefutura.

Pineda: Fulgencio Zuniga of Colombia was a constant comer with a hard punch and an iron chin. Pavlik had an impressive record of 26-0, including 23 knockouts. Pavlik, an unproven commodity at the pro level, was an exciting rising star in the sport, and the highest profile individual athlete from Ohio since Buster Douglas. A client of mine, from Youngstown, once told me their claim to fame is Bruce Springsteen writing a song ("Youngstown") about their town, and of course, being the hometown of boxing great Ray "Boom Boom" Mancini.

The bout started with Zuniga doing lots of moving around Pavlik who chose to stand steady in the center of the ring and try to catch his herky-jerky opponent.

At the midway point of the opening round, Pavlik caught Zuniga with a solid shot that rocked him. With 1:08 left in the round, Zuniga shocked Pavlik with a left hook that stung him, and followed up with another left hand that landed solid to the chin of Pavlik and sent him down. Referee Robert Byrd began the count, and Pavlik was up quickly, looking more surprised than hurt. He winked at someone in the audience while taking the mandatory 8-count. "The Ghost" finished the round looking strong, but had to defend against Zuniga's aggressive assault.

> **Pineda**: While as a fan I always look forward to a rising star being tested for the first time, almost nobody could have anticipated the early fireworks this night would provide. Pavlik, who had scored 19 of his 23 knockouts within two rounds, and immediately looked in total control with his height and reach and well-timed hard combinations, was the one who quickly found himself with his back on the canvas in the first, courtesy of a perfectly timed left hook by Zuniga, over his taller opponent's right hand. By the count of five, perhaps more embarrassed than hurt, Pavlik was up from being knocked down for the first time in 27 fights.

Round 2 saw Zuniga continue to catch Pavlik with wide left hands as Pavlik remained steady and fired back with hard counter shots. The fight settled into a pattern with Zuniga trying to lunge in and catch his opponent with wide shots from awkward angles. Kelly Pavlik continued in a steady methodical fashion, standing straight up and returning a mix of jab/right hand combinations and short counter shots. Pavlik looked more polished, much more styled in his boxing, yet Zuniga's awkward offensive attack was effective enough to make it a close bout throughout. It appeared to be a war of attrition that might be decided on who had the better stamina and ability to take punishment.

> **Pineda**: Zuniga came out that night as if he was double parked. He must have drunk a full coffee pot of potent Colombian coffee in his dressing room. In a high-pressure style that cancelled whatever his disadvantages in height and reach, he was effective with combinations and inside power shots in a true war of attrition.

It was round 6 that a change in the feeling of the match began. Zuniga seemed to be slowing down just a tad, and Pavlik's consistent power punching style began to take control. Even though Zuniga had demonstrated that he could knock Pavlik down in the opening round, that threat seemed to dissipate as the fight moved along. Zuniga's punches that landed didn't seem to bother his opponent, and Pavlik began walking through them and answering back. Though it seemed that Pavlik was starting to take command, it was not one-sided by any means. They both gave, they both took. A cut appeared over the left eye of Zuniga and his chief trainer, Orlando Pineda, went to work on it between rounds.

> **Pineda**: With Zuniga putting early pressure by going toe to toe, displaying stamina, footwork, and a strong chin, it took Pavlik seven action-packed rounds to decipher the Colombian warrior. His eight-inch reach advantage was not used much as the Ghost fought this one at close quarters, with fast inside combinations. After six very competitive rounds, Zuniga's face could not help but show signs of weariness, including a small cut as the pendulum swung in favor of the unbeaten Pavlik. After seven rounds, Zuniga was very visibly tired with the pace he himself set. His trainer said, "He doesn't want to anymore," which I perceived as Zuniga wanting to quit.

The two waged war in round 8 with a nearly full three minutes of inside fighting that was filled with hard exchanges. Heads were banging together while the two were rumbling at close quarters. A horrible cut had now opened over Zuniga's right eye with blood spilling all over his face, and the arms and torso of his opponent. Referee Robert Byrd called timeout with about 47 seconds left in the round, and motioned for the ring physician to assess the bleeding. The television microphone picked him up as he informed the commissioners at ringside that there were two cuts:

> **Byrd** (to the commissioners): The one on the right side is a punch. The one on the left side is a butt. Roll time, let's go, let's go!

The two went right back to work and finished the round with both fighters landing some heavy head shots.

They came out and touched gloves to start the ninth round. Zuniga's cuts were covered with globs of Vaseline in an attempt to block the flow of blood. It didn't take long for a Pavlik power punch to send the Vaseline flying, and the blood to again start flowing freely. Both fighters did what they do best, and that was to trade power punches. The two boxers looked worn down from a steady exchange of punishment. Even though it was Zuniga who was bleeding profusely, Pavlik's lighter colored skin showed the blood smeared all over the sides of his head and torso. At about the one-minute mark of the ninth round, Pavlik was splattered in Fulgencio Zuniga's blood. They just kept wailing away on each other. With about 25 seconds left in the round, Pavlik landed a shot that sent Zuniga stumbling backwards, rocked, but not close to going down from the punch.

This war was finally halted at the end of nine rounds, after Zuniga's two-inch cut kept bleeding into his right eye, causing him to take so many clean, hard shots.

The bell sounded, and referee Byrd walked over to the Zuniga corner, concerned about the condition of both the fighter and the two cuts over his eyes.

As Zuniga sat on the stool in his corner, cutman Rafael Garcia was seen waving his hands at the referee in a manner that looked clearly to say, "Stop the fight!" When referee asked if the fight was being stopped, Garcia, with a cotton swab sticking out of his mouth, was nodding "yes," but Zuniga's head trainer was insisting that it had not been stopped.

> **Pineda**: The controversy and confusion ensued after Zuniga's cut man, Rafael Garcia, asked the doctor to stop it, without the head trainer, Orlando Pineda, being aware. The controversy started when the trainer protested the stoppage, only to be told it was too late to change the outcome. Looking at what was starting to happen, you can't fault the cutman for wanting to end it.

The confusion heated up as the referee tried to get a clear understanding of what the corner wanted to do. One of the deputy inspectors standing on the ring apron informed Byrd that Rafael Garcia had repeatedly said "alto" ("stop") as he waved his hands. The inspector pointed right at Garcia and said, "He said alto." But as head trainer Pineda said that the fight was not being stopped, Garcia began treating the cuts over the eyes of his fighter.

As Garcia seemed to sense that he may have made a mistake, the ring physician, referee, and deputy inspector were all shouting out their interpretation of what was indicated by the cornermen. The inspector repeatedly pointed at the cutman saying, "He said alto, he said alto." Garcia, dressed in a white shirt, with his beanie cap festooned in colorful pins, looked confused and gently shook his head "no." Pineda, dressed in a black shirt, was firm in saying that the fight was not being stopped.

Byrd made sure he understood as he pointed at Rafael Garcia, and asked the commissioner straight out if Garcia stopped the fight. The inspector made it clear as he pointed directly at Garcia and said, "Yes, he said alto, he stopped the fight." But Pineda said the fight was not being stopped. The inspector firmly said, "Too late, too late, stop, stop!"

The referee immediately went out to the center of the ring and waved his hands over his head, indicating that the fight had been stopped. Pavlik's fans began cheering "Kel-ly! Kel-ly! Kel-ly!"

Things then heated up as Zuniga's chief second insisted that the fight was going to continue, but the decision had already been made, the fight was being stopped.

Pineda angrily protested as the inspector continued to make it clear that cutman Garcia had called for the fight to be stopped. Pineda barked at the deputy inspector:

Inspector: He said alto, he said alto.

Pineda: I am principal. I am the principal!

Inspector: He said alto, he said alto.

Pineda: You! You say, I stop it, you say I stop it!

Inspector: No, he said to stop it [pointing at Garcia].

The Telemundo broadcast crew tried to sort things out, and a replay of what was going on in the corner was shown to the worldwide audience to show exactly what was being said.

The replay clearly showed the ring physician come in and ask the chief trainer, "Are you guys stopping it?" Pineda wasn't clear with his response, and then Garcia nodded and waved his hand, as the deputy inspector instructed the physician that the fight was being stopped. Garcia, realizing that he may have acted prematurely, then said, "Let him go." The inspector said, "Too late. Stop." Garcia had to feel terrible as both the ring doctor and the inspector pointed at him, saying "He said stop." Referee Byrd then made a final clarification and pointed at Garcia and asked, "He stopped it?" and all heads shook in the affirmative.

Pavlik's cutman, Miguel Diaz, came over to the Zuniga corner and tried to be helpful in sorting things out. Zuniga just sat in his corner looking resigned to the situation.

As it turns out, Pavlik would have won whether the corner stopped it, or if it had been stopped by the referee for the cut caused by the head butt requiring that they go to the scorecards, as he was ahead on all three judges' scorecards by scores of 88–83, 87–83, and 87–83 at the time of the stoppage.

> **Pineda**: At the end of the night, by making adjustments like keeping his right hand up, putting combinations together, using his speed, reach advantage, and bodyshots, this was the night that Pavlik proved himself at the contender level in the middleweight division and worthy to challenge Jermain Taylor for the world middleweight belt, the man he would go on to defeat.

Telemundo's Ricardo Celis went into the ring and interviewed Garcia, Pineda, and Zuniga about the way the fight ended. First up was the man at the center of the firestorm, cutman Rafael Garcia, who explained that he did indeed feel that the fight should be stopped because of the wide open and dangerous cuts sustained by his fighter.

> **Pineda**: I can't help but think how in boxing, machismo and saving face are almost as important as the actual outcome, for a fighter, at least. In this instance, part of it looked to me as if the cutman played good cop to the head trainer's bad cop. Yet, cutman Garcia sounded very sincere in his explanation of why he stopped it, concern over his fighter's safety.

Zuniga's chief trainer, Orlando Pineda, made it clear that he was upset because he was the chief trainer, and did not want the fight stopped. He felt it was the deputy inspector of the Nevada Boxing Commission who actually stopped the fight—a fight *he* did not want stopped. Zuniga felt that he was doing good in the fight and was probably in an even fight, or up by a point or two. He said that he expected to score a knockout by the eleventh or twelfth round. The trio seemed to be calm and united, and there did not appear to be any bad blood between the head trainer, the fighter, and their cutman.

Pavlik fought for about seven more years, defending his NABF middleweight title twice, and winning both the WBC and WBO middleweight world titles.

> **Pineda**: Looking back at this match, and its back-and-forth wild action and unpredictable nature, one can see parallels with how Pavlik's life would turn out to be outside of the ring, from the wacky to the controversial. After his title winning fight with Jermain Taylor, Pavlik and his father accidentally left their paychecks in their hotel room. He once refused to pay a cab fare, was arrested for assault at a Foo Fighters concert, and shot a worker with a pellet gun while he was digging a lake at his home.

Zuniga continued fighting, making several world title challenges, and was still active as this book went to press in 2017.

CHAPTER TWELVE

Out, But Not Out

Allen Conyers vs. Delvin Rodriguez

August 24, 2004
Poughkeepsie, New York

On an ESPN2 televised event held at the Mid-Hudson Civic Center, one of the undercard bouts featured two up-and-coming welterweights. Unbeaten Allen Conyers came in with a record of 8–0, and 6 KOs. The Bronx fighter was looking to continue his unbeaten ring career with a win over a fellow prospect, Connecticut's Delvin Rodriguez, 11–1–1, 6 by KO.

The bout got off to a confused start before the first bell even rang. During the ring introductions, ESPN2 placed Conyer's name and information over a close-up of Delvin Rodriguez, and the same happened when they flashed Rodriguez's information for Conyers. When ESPN2's broadcaster Joe Tessitore noticed the mistake on his TV monitor, he said:

> **Tessitore**: Actually, *that* is Allen Conyers, right there. Disregard the Delvin Rodriguez note there.

As the ring intros finished up, and referee Eddie Claudio waited for the first bell, an official at the ringside table stood up to get his attention, telling him that the two fighters needed to switch corners. Claudio immediately instructed the two boxers to switch positions, and then waited for the two corners to gather up all of their gear and make their way around the aisle to the opposite corners. While waiting for the two teams to make their way over to the new corners, the broadcasters added:

> **Tessitore**: You know at the end of the day, Scott, the bottom line is, they have to have a fight.

> **LeDoux**: At the end of the day, it doesn't matter what corner they come out of, it's how they fight.

While the cameras showed the parade of cornermen working their way around the aisles, the team quipped:

> **Tessitore**: And, the delay now, maybe you can see right there, as the corners, and the chief seconds, spit bucket, cutmen, they have to make their way around the square.
>
> **LeDoux**: At least they didn't call Beacons or somebody to move them.

The fight finally got under way, with both working behind jabs. Conyers danced his way in and out while moving to his left. Rodriguez took control of the center of the ring.

The two lean welterweights showed nice hand speed, good skill, and appeared to be well matched.

Round 2 was fought evenly, but Conyers landed a big left hook that snapped the head of Rodriguez, possibly making the difference to give him, what was to that point, a close round.

The two continued to struggle evenly for the next two rounds, each having their moments in what became a tactical boxing match. Conyers got off to the better start, but you could feel the momentum move slowly toward Rodriguez.

The fifth round saw the same pattern early, but in the final minute Rodriguez was starting to catch Conyers with some straight, hard shots. With 10 seconds to go in the round, Rodriguez connected with a right hand that, for just an instant, froze Conyers, followed by a short left that connected, and then a left hand that cuffed the stunned fighter, causing him to stumble back and out of the ring. Conyers went right over the bottom rope and down to the arena floor. It was a freaky sight as Conyers landed on the floor, and for a second he remained face down, with his legs stiff, and the lace portion of his white shoes hanging over the bottom rope. Some gentlemen moved the table back so that he could get up, a few tried to assist him, but an official with the state athletic commission seemed to be telling them that they could not help him back into the ring. Referee Claudio began the count. Conyers climbed up the steps, and through the ropes, just beating the count as the bell sounded ending this wild round.

The ESPN2 broadcast team were impressed with the whole scene as they focused on the monitors in front of them:

> **Tessitore**: Out of the ring goes Allen Conyers! Holy cow! Delvin Rodriguez put him out of the ring! He's got to beat that count, and he does! Have you ever seen that? He continues on from out of the ring! What is this? The WWF? Wow! Delvin Rodriguez floors Allen Conyers, literally floors him!
>
> **LeDoux**: Unbelievable. He just takes it to him. Firing shots, Rodriguez was throwing straight, straight punches, caught him with two hooks, out the ropes he went!

With the crowd standing on their feet, screaming with excitement, the next round started with Joe Tessitore declaring:

> **Tessitore**: We head to the sixth and final round. Visions of Louie Firpo and Jack Dempsey. The sportswriters didn't help Allen Conyers back into the ring, he did it on his own. And give him tons of credit for even getting back up on the apron, going through the ropes, and beating the 10-count. How many times have you ever seen that?

Meanwhile, Conyer's trainer—former world Champion James Buddy McGirt—*accidentally* spilled the ice bucket on the mat, which gave his fighter a little additional time to recover as he wiped up the water. It brought the crowd alive, and delighted fans around the world tuned in on ESPN2.

The two boxers, being the professionals that they were, went right back to work. If you tuned in to the fight at this point, you wouldn't have had a clue that anything unusual had just happened. The fight pattern fell into place. Conyers jabbing and moving forward, Rodriguez stepping and shooting counter punches. With 22 seconds to go in the fight, Rodriguez laid against the ropes as Conyers leaned in on him, putting all of his weight on Rodriguez. With 10 seconds left it happened again, causing the referee to call a time out and admonish Conyers for the tactic. The bell sounded, and the fight went to the scorecards of the three judges.

The final punch stats were very close, nearly identical, showing Rodriguez throwing eight more punches, and landing one more punch, with Conyers holding a 1% edge in accuracy. But punch stats don't always tell the whole story, and Scott LeDoux's unofficial scorecard had Rodriguez winning 58–55 aided by that big fifth round.

Ring announcer Kent Bonham was certainly impressed as he interjected to the crowd before reading the scores: "What an amazing fight, let's give it up for both fighters tonight. Wow, impressive fight tonight!"

The official scores were 59–54 across the board in favor of Connecticut's Delvin Rodriguez.

Allen Conyers battled on for about a decade, fighting for the USBA welterweight title and winning the New York State welterweight title.

Delvin Rodriguez was still active as a professional boxer as of this writing. He went on to win the USBA welterweight championship, and fought in three world-title challenges.

CHAPTER THIRTEEN

Pugilistic Breakdown

Lennox Lewis vs. Oliver McCall II

February 7, 1997
Las Vegas, Nevada

It was one of the strangest sights ever seen during a boxing match. WBC heavyweight champion Oliver McCall was fighting a rematch with the man he upset to gain that title. Just 2½ years earlier, McCall had traveled to London where he scored a huge upset over undefeated world champion Lennox Lewis. He had defended his title in a close decision over Larry Holmes, but lost it to British sensation Frank Bruno in the second defense of his title, nearly a year after winning the belt.

Since losing his title belt to McCall, Lennox Lewis had mowed down three opponents by knockout, including Tommy "The Duke" Morrison, and then scored a close majority decision win to earn a shot at the now-vacant WBC title belt. Lewis wanted his belt back. McCall was determined to prove that the first win over Lewis was not a fluke.

The crowd sensed something brewing. McCall had won the coin flip, entitling him to enter the ring last. During his introduction, he started running to the ring, with his entourage chasing after him. He literally jumped over the steps leading up into the ring, going from floor to ring canvas in a single bound. Climbing through the ropes, he began bouncing around, pacing back and forth, hyped up and ready to go. Across the ring, Lennox Lewis stood stoic and serious with an emotionless look on his face.

As the two were brought to the center of the ring by the referee, Mills Lane, Lewis stood statue still, not even blinking.

McCall was swinging back and forth, side to side, looking agitated. They did not touch gloves before returning to their corners. World championship boxing judge and boxrec.com editor Nathan Palmer remembers it well:

> **Palmer**: McCall-Lewis 2. With the exception of the Fan Man, this may very well be the strangest thing I've ever seen in boxing. Oliver basically had all the psychological advantages going into this fight. He had already beaten Lewis. Cleanly knocked him out. So going into this, I'm thinking this is going to be a great fight.

As the bout started in round 1, McCall came out quick and scored well, but was soon tamed by the Lewis jab. Round 2 saw Lewis begin to connect with some wicked uppercuts and right hands. Round 3 saw a change in the body language of McCall who began mugging and shrugging his shoulders during the round.

> **Palmer**: Bell rings, it's not a particularly good fight at all. As the rounds go on you can tell there's something wrong with Oliver. He's just not fighting. Not the most uncommon thing in boxing, but one that makes for a very dull fight nonetheless.

It was between rounds three and four that things started to go south. Rather than sitting in his corner to let his team work on him, McCall wandered around the ring looking out into the crowd as his trainer and corner men stood with a disgusted and confused look on their faces. The legendary George Benton was the chief trainer, and he looked totally frustrated. McCall wandered around for the entire minute rest period. When the bell rang, he walked out to meet Lewis, but looked lethargic and disinterested. Lewis surely sensed the change, and seemed a little confused himself, He continued to box cautiously, but effectively. The audience wasn't sure what to make of it.

During the round, HBO's Larry Merchant took a microphone to talk with McCall's trainer, George Benton, who said "This man's mind is gone. Have you ever seen anything like this in your life?" Merchant asked him if there were any signs of trouble before the fight. Benton's answer was simple: "Nothing."

When the bell to end round 4 sounded, McCall continued to pace around, and began weeping as his trainers got him to sit down. It was a totally bizarre scene. Referee Lane asked him if he wanted to continue fighting, and he shook his head in the affirmative. The fifth round started with Lennox Lewis placed in a very awkward position, not sure whether to put his arm around McCall and say "There, there, it will be alright," or punch him in the jaw and knock him out. He didn't have much choice and threw a few hard shots, with no resistance from McCall. Lane had seen enough and waved off the fight. It was announced as a technical knockout, but went into the record books as a disqualification at 55 seconds of round 5.

> **Palmer**: Eventually it becomes very clear he is having a psychological breakdown that has nothing to do with boxing. He's flat out refusing to fight. He's breaking down in tears. He does not want to be there. Not out of fear. He's never even been knocked down. This isn't exactly a guy who has ever quivered at the sight of another man across the ring from him. Something is wrong. This fight is over.

The executive director of the Nevada State Athletic Commission, Mark Ratner, expressed his displeasure with the performance of McCall, saying that there would be an investigation, and a with-holding of McCall's sizeable purse.

During a post-fight interview, the new world heavyweight champion, Lennox Lewis, expressed his thoughts:

> **Lewis**: I thought it was a joke or something, or that he was trying to lull me into something.

Lewis' trainer, Emanuel Steward, added:

> **Steward**: He [McCall] is just a high-strung emotional guy, he just said, "Forget it."

This was not the end of the line for the fighter known as "The Atomic Bull," not by a longshot. McCall would recover from this debacle and put together a 13-fight win streak including 11 knockouts over some decent opposition, including a tenth-round knockout win over former WBO and WBC heavyweight world champion Henry Akinwande. McCall fought for 11 more years after that strange night in Las Vegas.

> **Palmer**: The one guy who beat Lennox and Lennox never really got to avenge it. A win on paper alone. Who knows, maybe McCall was the guy to have Lennox's number.

Lennox Lewis went on to a glorious career, and is a member of the International Boxing Hall of Fame.

CHAPTER FOURTEEN

I Am from Long Beach!

Attila Levin vs. Jeremy Williams

April 15, 2004
New York, New York

Heavyweight Jeremy Williams brought his record of 40–4–1, 34 wins by KO, to the Hammerstein Ballroom for a fight against up-and-comer Attila Levin, who was 29–1, with 23 by KO.

It was almost four years since Levin had been shocked by an opponent who stopped him in one round in the same building, and it had been nearly four years since Williams had lost a boxing match, too. So this was an anticipated match-up with title contention implications. It was the night's main event of a card broadcast on Showtime. One of the best ring announcers in the business, "Generous" Joe Antonacci, was doing the introductions. He remembers it well:

> **Antonacci**: I had to go with the New York State Athletic Commission's hometown info because Williams was late arriving and the card had started. Jimmy Hoffa Jr., Al Sharpton, etc., were there that night promoting the ill-fated boxer's union (JAB) so it was packed. Jimmy Lennon Sr.'s #1 rule for ring announcers was to get there early to speak with the fighters and get their preferred home towns, nicknames, name pronunciations, etc. straight from their mouths. They also sometimes switch trunk colors from what they may have told you or the commission at the weigh-in the day before.

He introduced the officials for the bout, in his smooth announcing style. And then the fighters, Jeremy Williams in the blue corner, first. He introduced this gentleman, describing his trunks, height, weight, his record, it was all right on, until he got to Jeremy's home town: "...from Sherman Oaks, California, by way of Fort Dodge, Idaho..."

That's when Williams lowered his brow and shook his head. He approached Antonacci and more than tapped him in the belly with his gloved hand, saying "I'm from Long Beach!" Antonacci tried to play it cool and continue, when another tap, bordering on a light punch, on the torso from Williams came along with another stern, "I'm from Long Beach!"

> **Antonacci**: When I said Sherman Oaks (a wealthy town he had "moved up" to), he and his team first just said "Long Beach." When I kept going and didn't correct the town, he walked from his corner to center ring and tapped me on the chest (hard; not a love tap) and said "Long Beach," at which point I said, "From Long Beach, California." He was clearly pissed. It was a TV fight and I had inadvertently destroyed his street cred in his mind.

Antonacci finished the intro with: "Jeremy Half-Man, Half-Amazing, Williams!" Williams appeared satisfied with the correction and returned to his corner as Antonacci finished his introductions. It was a lesson that has helped to form the ring announcing style of one of boxing's top announcers.

> **Antonacci**: Since then, if a fighter is late, preventing me from meeting them, I ask their chief second (in the ring) to confirm the hometown and nickname. I also check the trunks.

Jeremy Williams went on to stop Levin in round 8. The announcement of the decision was very clear: "2 minutes, and 48 seconds into the eighth round, on the advice of the doctor at ringside, our referee stops the contest. Your winner from *Long Beach*, California, Jeremy 'Half Man, Half Amazing' Williams!"

The Williams fans from Long Beach, California, were never more proud. I was from South Gate, just 16 miles up the road from Long Beach, but I was proud, too—of both Williams *and* "Generous Joe."

CHAPTER FIFTEEN

The Fan Man

Riddick Bowe vs. Evander Holyfield II

November 6, 1993
Las Vegas, Nevada

A heavyweight world title bout for both the IBF and WBA titles headlines an outdoor event staged at Caesar's Palace. The combatants had met nearly one year earlier, with Riddick Bowe handing Evander Holyfield his first professional defeat and lifting the unified heavyweight title from around his waist. "Bad" Brad Berkwitt, author of *Boxing Interviews of a Lifetime*, and CEO/publisher of RingsideReport.com, recalls:

> **Berkwitt**: I watched Holyfield vs Bowe I and was rooting for Riddick to win. It was a fight party with a bunch of my Navy pals and what a great fight that was. I felt this was the finest night in Bowe's career; he took the fight very seriously. He had two very weak opponents in Jesse Ferguson and Michael Dokes that he defended against and who did nothing for his career. But now, after Dokes, we have Bowe vs Holyfield II.

Bowe entered the ring with a perfect 34–0 record, and was making his third defense of the heavyweight title. After an impressive win in his first meeting with Holyfield, Bowe scored a first-round TKO and second-round KO in his next two title bouts. Holyfield returned from his first defeat to score a 12-round unanimous decision over Alex "Destroyer" Stewart.

Both boxers came in quite a bit heavier than they were in their first meeting. Bowe was 11 pounds heavier this time around, Holyfield was 12 pounds heavier. Bowe maintained his size advantage, weighing in at 246 pounds, a 29-pound difference over the former champion who came in at 217 pounds. Most saw the increase as an advantage for Holyfield who, many imagined, was in better physical condition for this meeting, appearing to have added muscle mass, not fat.

> **Berkwitt**: Bowe, though still tough, started showing how lazy he was in his training, a problem that would follow him for the rest of his career. As they said in the movie *A Bronx Tale*, "The saddest thing in life is wasted talent, and the choices that you make will shape your life forever!"

The first four rounds were even. Holyfield was staying busy and trying to impose his offensive skills on the bigger champion. Bowe seemed content to work behind his jab and let Holyfield wear down.

It was an intense match with the two fighters continuing to fight after the bell in round 4. Trainer Emanuel Stewart jumped in to pull Holyfield away, while referee Mills Lane struggled to pull the two boxes apart as a commission official jumped in to assist in breaking up the two and getting them back to their respective corners. The fight was on!

Bowe had a cut over his left eye and a cut between the eyes. Nothing too serious, but enough to concern his cutman.

Broadcaster Jim Lampley noted that Bowe had been stunned at the end of round 5 by a huge left-right combination from Evander Holyfield:

> **Lampley**: And the round comes to a close,the bell saving Riddick Bowe from further punishment!

After six rounds, controversy was brewing as HBO's unofficial scorecard penned by Harold Lederman showed Bowe ahead 58–56. Broadcaster Larry Merchant completely disagreed:

> **Merchant**: Controversy or not, Harold, you and I couldn't disagree more. I have Evander Holyfield ahead 4 rounds to 1, and 1 even.

Either way, it was a competitive bout which felt like Holyfield may have been starting to take command.

With about 1:58 left in round 7, you could hear a change in the sound of the crowd as they noticed a huge object falling out of the sky and landing on the corner ring apron. As the two were locked in battle, Holyfield looked up over the crouched Riddick Bowe and stepped back in stunned disbelief while Mills Lane signaled for a time out. Bowe turned around to see a man in some kind of contraption, dressed in an orange jump suit wearing a white helmet, falling off of the ring apron and being dragged away from the ring in a chaotic scene that words could hardly describe. Brad Berkwitt remembers it well:

> **Berkwitt**: Bowe was doing good until the Fan Man decided to bring his crazy butt into the ring which shocked my pals and I who were watching the fight. As you know, they stopped it for I think over 30 minutes and it changed the outcome of the fight where Holyfield got back into it.

The rope lines from the parachute were hung up on a huge bank of lights set up for the PPV broadcast. The crash landing took place in the Bowe corner, and the "pilot" was immediately met with an assault of Bowe's handlers along with Caesar's security guards. The man and his flying machine were dragged off of the ring apron, and he was getting pummeled before being taken into immediate custody. Service workers went right to work trying to clear the parachute and all of the attachments to it off of the ring lights in hopes of getting this long-awaited world heavyweight title fight back into action.

California boxing fan Rene Ramirez recalls:

> **Ramirez**: I saw the Holyfield fight on PPV. What a great night of boxing that was. We were all in shock when Fan Man arrived...then saw them beat the crap out of him.

The HBO camera crew had spotted the intruder as he glided around the skies above the ring, but were probably not thinking that he would try to land in the ring area. Footage was shown of the paraglider cruising along the night sky before making its final descent. The "Fan Man" was James Miller, a 29-year-old parachutist. After he landed, he was beaten nearly unconscious and then taken to a nearby hospital, before being booked, charged a $200 fine, and released.

While things were getting sorted out, Bowe's corner smartly used that time to work on his cuts, and did their best to keep him warm. Holyfield's corner probably felt that their man was in control, and this break in momentum could change things.

It was such a surreal scene. Those present weren't sure exactly what had just happened and what it meant, especially those in the seats closest to the whole scene as it unfolded. Was it a threat to their safety? Was it some kind of gimmick? Fans watching the pay-per-view broadcast at home were equally puzzled. I know everyone in my household on that night buzzed about it for hours.

After all of the chaos was brought to order, the bout continued to its conclusion, going the distance, and it was a close one. The judges' scorecards read 114–114 even, and 115–114 and 115-113 in favor of the winner by a razor-thin majority decision, Evander Holyfield. "The Real Deal" Holyfield had regained two (IBF and WBA) of the heavyweight titles and returned the favor, handing Riddick Bowe *his* first and, as it turned out, only career loss.

> **Berkwitt**: It was a great fight and the scores showed just how close when they were announced. I think had the Fan Man not come in the ring, Bowe would have pulled out the fight. After this fight, Bowe would get even worse with his training regime.

Two years later, these two would meet for a non-title rubber match with Riddick Bowe stopping Holyfield in eight rounds. They both continued on with glorious careers.

> **Berkwitt**: To his credit, even with horrible training habits, Bowe won the WBO heavyweight belt against Herbie Hide and defended it once against Jorge Luis Gonzalez. Though he won all his fights after Holyfield vs Bowe II against some outstanding and some poor opposition, his fire was never there again in his boxing career. It's a shame because had he lived up to his full potential I always felt he could have been one of the best big heavyweights ever.

Evander Holyfield would go on to fight 26 more bouts, including historic matches with Mike Tyson, Michael Moorer, Lennox Lewis, a trilogy of fights with John Ruiz, and many other big names of the heavyweight division. Bowe would fight 10 more times without losing another bout, including his famous set of bouts with Andrew Golota.

CHAPTER SIXTEEN

Bolted-Down Chairs Are Best

Marco Antonio Avendano vs. Sebastian Lujan

December 17, 2005
Rosario, Argentina

In a Saturday night card at the Club El Ciclon, local favorite Sebastian "Iron" Lujan (24–2–2, 16 KO) was matched up against Venezuelan Marco Antonio Avendano (20–5–1, 13 KO), with the vacant WBA Fedalatin welterweight title up for grabs. The title bout was scheduled for 12 rounds.

Things started pretty fast as the pride of Argentina, Lujan, came out as the aggressor and chased Avendano into the ropes, landing a nice left hand to the head and right hand to the body combination, and repeating it to score well and get the crowd fired up. Again, he chased Avendano into the corner and fired away landing some solid shots bringing a rise out of the crowd. The final 45 seconds of the round ticked away with Lujan landing a bomb to the head of Avendano, but Avendano retaliated as Lujan just tied him up and looked out at the crowd with a look of complete confidence. Lujan made Avendano retreat every time he moved ahead throwing punches. The bell sounded with Avendano in retreat, and it looked like a great night for the Argentinian fighter. The crowd was pleased.

Round 2 started out with Lujan pinning Avendano in the corner and going to work when suddenly Avendano landed a right-hand counter that saw the Argentine fall flat on his back. He was back on his feet by the count of 5, but wobbled around the ring, not looking steady. It seemed like a pretty slow count, and the ref seemed to be giving the local guy as much time as he could milk out of the 8-count. The bout continued and Avendano was like a shark that smelled blood in the water. He came in and opened up with non-stop punching as Lujan tried to bob and weave his way out of trouble, but getting caught with most of the shots. Just as the referee jumped in to give him a standing 8-count, he fell to the canvas and the ref started the count. The crowd that was celebrating in round 1 now felt concern in round 2 as the referee continued the slow-motion count. When he reached 8, Lujan raised his gloves as if to say. "I'm OK," but the referee shook his head "no" and waved the fight off as he hugged Lujan. The fight was over and the local guy was the loser. A TKO win for the Venezuelan fighter, Avendano, with an official time of 1:25 in round 2.

Avendano was happy and ran around the ring with his trainer celebrating, but he must have forgotten where he was as he turned to Lujan and gave him the "humping gesture" with his outstretched fists and hip thrusts.

That was all it took to turn the crowd into a raging mob. Being a night club, there were no permanent seats, it was all plastic patio-type chairs and the fans were not in the mood for sitting any longer. The chairs started flying into the ring. Avendano's trainer proudly held his man's gloved hand in the air until a plastic chair nailed him, and they made their way out of the ring fast, keeping their heads down and covered as they ran to the locker room.

After the crowd realized that their targets had fled, the official announcement of the winner was made by the ring announcer, by which time Avendano was probably sneaking out to his car without a shower. Just mail the check.

CHAPTER SEVENTEEN

After the Bell?

Tomas Molinares vs. Marlon Starling

July 29, 1988
Atlantic City, New Jersey

This was a memorable fight not because a huge upset *had* (apparently) taken place, but *how* it happened.

WBA welterweight champion Marlon "Magic Man" Starling was defending his title against unbeaten, but untested contender Tomas Molinares of Colombia.

Starling was one of the best welterweights of his time—slick and tricky, quick and hard to catch, a tight defense, and enough offense to get the job done against anyone. He had handed champion Mark Breland his first defeat and took the WBA title belt. In his next two bouts, he defeated Fujio Ozaki, and fought a 12-round draw with Breland in their rematch.

Molinares was 22-0, but had fought outside of Colombia only once during his career.

The thing that stood out about this match was the ages of the two fighters. Starling was nearly 30 years old, while his Colombian challenger was only 23 years old. And Molinares did have 19 knockouts in 22 fights. No one doubted that he was untested, but he was still considered a threat.

Starling was a clear favorite, and with WBC welterweight champion Lloyd "Honey" Honeyghan fighting on the same card, it was considered a "showcase" for those two champions. If they won, they would possibly meet in a unification bout later that year, or early the next year.

Honeyghan fought the first of the two co-main events, scoring a fifth-round TKO over South Korea's Yung-Kil Chung for the seventh successful defense of his WBC title belt. Now it was Starling's turn to hold up his end of the play.

The bout turned tactical right away as Molinares showed good skills and stayed busy with his jab. Starling's defense was tight, with that high hands "peek-a-boo" style. The two pecked away at each other with their jabs, scoring with an occasional power punch in a close fight through five rounds. It was the last minute of round 5 that Starling started to score with flashy combinations and looked like his championship skills would start to pull him ahead in the scoring. When Starling returned to his corner, head trainer Eddie Futch was very pleased with the way his man had started to perform in that round.

Round 6 saw the champion starting to assert himself with strong punches and putting on effective pressure against his young opponent. The two were fighting on the outside mostly, as referee Joe Cortez hardly had to separate the two fighters. Cortez's job would get quite a bit harder at the end of this round.

As the two were in an exchange, the bell sounded, and an instant after the bell Molinares connected with a huge overhand right that sent Starling to the canvas, his body stretched out. Referee Cortez had to make an instant decision, and decided to begin the count. Starling struggled to get up off of the canvas. He crawled to his knees and gloves, but did not beat the count. It was a solid knockout punch.

Boxing referee and historian Vic de Wysocki remembers:

> **Wysocki**: I remember watching this tightly contested 1988 WBA welterweight title fight where challenger Tomas Molinares unintentionally landed a knockout punch just after the bell sounds to end the sixth round and veteran referee Joe Cortez counted champion Marlon Starling out.

Tomas Molinares ran around the ring jumping and falling on his back as his trainers hugged him in celebration. Meanwhile, Starling was helped to a stool and tended to by the ring doctor and his handlers.

There was a question as to whether the punch was launched before or after the bell. The HBO broadcast crew of Jim

Lampley, Larry Merchant, and Sugar Ray Leonard were all uncertain about what the official ruling would be.

Meanwhile, Starling sat on a stool surrounded by handlers and officials, looking around and unsure of what just happened.

Ring announcer Michael Buffer told the crowd:

> **Buffer**: Ladies and gentlemen, your attention, please. Referee Joe Cortez rules that the final punch was thrown as the bell rang. A fighter cannot be saved by the bell. The count continues, the winner and new champion from Barranquilla, Colombia—Tomas Molinares!

Boos erupted from the crowd who felt that the punch came after the bell, and the knockout should not have happened.

Cortez said that he felt the punch was launched as the bell rang, and landed after the bell, so the count should continue.

Starling's handlers immediately notified anyone within earshot that they would file a protest with the WBA and the New Jersey State Athletic Commission.

Molinares stated in Spanish that the punch was launched before the bell sounded. To add insult to injury, Starling's leg was injured when he fell and his handlers began wrapping the leg and ordered a stretcher to the ring on which to carry Starling back to the locker room. The proud champion insisted that he would *not* be carried out on a stretcher.

During the post-fight interview with HBO's Larry Merchant, Starling seemed not to be sure about what had just happened. Starling said that he heard the bell ring, and he twisted his leg.

Starling and Merchant had a fascinating exchange during the post-fight interview:

> **Merchant**: The referee has ruled...

Before finishing, he was cut off by the former champion seated on a stool.

> **Starling**: He counted me out? Was I out? When did he count? When?
>
> **Merchant**: Marlon, he did hit you. And if you don't remember it, that's proof that he hit you. But the dispute is whether he hit you as the bell rang, or after the bell rang ... and they stopped the fight because they counted you out, and they ruled that you were knocked out.

> **Starling**: Do I look knocked out? Do I look like I'm wobbled?
>
> **Merchant**: Well, you only have to be knocked out for 10 seconds.
>
> **Starling**: I wasn't knocked out, I wasn't knocked *down*!

A bizarre exchange indeed.

The chairman of the New Jersey Athletic Commission, Larry Hazzard, was allowed to look at a videotape replay of the knockout, and was asked by Jim Lampley what he saw. He stated that the punch was in motion when the bell rang, and that the ruling would stand. The rule "protect yourself at all times" was repeated over and over at ringside.

The scorecards after five rounds showed a very close fight, with Starling up by one point on two of the cards, and a 48–48 even scorecard. The sixth round was not scored.

Larry Merchant's term "the theater of the unexpected" was never more true than this night. And in another unexpected twist after all of the controversy, and a further review, the decision was changed from a TKO win for Molinares, to a no contest. Molinares' reign as champion was short lived.

> **Wysocki**: The silver lining in this unfortunate situation was the advent of the "10-second warning sound" that is now heard just before each round ends in a professional boxing match, thus alerting both the boxers and referee that the round is about to end. Its implementation has since greatly reduced the likelihood that an errant punch will be thrown after the bell sounds to end a round, something I as a referee have no doubt benefited from.

Whatever the decision, it did not derail Marlon Starling's career, as he went on just seven months later to stop WBC champion Lloyd Honeyghan in the ninth round, winning the WBC world welterweight title, and further cementing his status as a great champion.

It seemed to take much more out of Tomas Molinares, who was knocked out in the early rounds of his next two fights, both in Barranquilla, Colombia, and then never fought again.

CHAPTER EIGHTEEN

Fight of the Year (An Acoustic Decision)

Iran Barkley vs. Roberto Duran

February 24, 1989
Atlantic City, New Jersey

The Atlantic City Convention Center was the venue for this much-anticipated meeting between the newly crowned WBC middleweight champion of the world, Iran "The Blade" Barkley, making his first defense of the title he had taken in shocking fashion from Thomas Hearns by knockout. The challenger was 37-year-old legend "Hands of Stone" Roberto Duran.

The smart money was on Barkley going in to this fight. He was nearly half-a-foot taller, had a nearly six-inch reach advantage, was three pounds heavier at the weigh-in, nine years younger, and he was the champion. He had all of the checks in his column. Duran still had a solid fan base, and even though he had not been involved in a "mega-fight" since being left face down in two rounds against Thomas Hearns 4½ years earlier, judging by the cheers of the crowd, he was their favorite, if not a favorite with the sports books. Former New York State Athletic Commission Chairman Randy Gordon recalls:

> **Gordon**: There was a blizzard raging along the northeast corridor of the U. S., and nowhere was it coming down harder than in Atlantic City. But even the blizzard of snow couldn't compare to the ferocity of the blizzard of punches middleweight champion Iran Barkley and challenger Roberto Duran were about to toss at each other in Atlantic City.

Duran entered the ring at 156¼ pounds. He looked fit and focused for this challenge. Barkley weighed in 159½, just under the 160-pound middleweight limit. Even though Barkley was the much bigger man on paper, when they were physically engaged in the ring, it did not appear to be a "David vs. Goliath" challenge for Duran, who wasn't dwarfed by the champion.

Joe Cortez, the referee, got his first test when the two fighters walked away from the pre-fight instructions at center ring without touching gloves. Cortez called them back to the ring with the broadcast microphone picking him up pleading with the two to touch gloves:

> **Cortez**: Shake hands now, good luck ... c'mon, c'mon, c'mon, c'mon, hey, c'mon. Iran! Hey, c'mon, shake hands, c'mon ... shake hands, all right, let's go!

They finally met at center ring and tapped gloves.

The house was completely packed, not an empty seat to be found. Duran's fans were delighted to see their hero get off to a great start, looking like the Duran of old with great feints and beautiful counter punching. Barkley smartly got his jab going right away, making the most of his sizable reach advantage.

With just 10 seconds left in the opening round, Duran landed a big right hand to the side of Barkley's head, right on the ear, that staggered him. The champion fell back and immediately grabbed Duran around the neck to ride out the final ticks of the clock to end the round. The bell sounded, and as the crowd rose to their feet in unison, Barkley walked with a shaky stride back to his corner, nodding in acknowledgment that he had indeed been hit by the hands of stone.

The two styles meshed well, and made for an entertaining battle. The fight went back and forth with both boxers doing some great work, and dishing out plenty of punishment. Barkley landed a pair of left hands that stung Duran who just kept working. It was a classic boxing moment as the bell sounded to end the seventh round: the two stood glaring at each other with Cortez between them with his hands outstretched. That scene lasted only a few seconds, but it was classic.

Round 8 saw the two giving and taking, when out of nowhere, Barkley landed a solid left hook, and a few seconds later landed a huge left hook that spun Duran and nearly sent him to the canvas. The experience of the legendary Duran showed as he was able to stay calm, continue working, and clear his head. It did appear that Duran was starting to wear down, but he kept going as the two exchanged head and body shots.

To start the ninth round, the broadcast team of Al Bernstein and Gil Clancy agreed that they had Barkley ahead in the fight. Bernstein wisely asked:

> **Bernstein**: Will the reputation of Roberto Duran mean anything to the judges, though? A question to be asked.

This was the round when Duran seemed to gain momentum, with the crowd raising chants of "Doo-ran! Doo-ran!" The Panamanian legend continued to work behind a well-timed jab and strong counter punches. It was a good round for Duran.

The tenth round ended with the broadcast team commenting on Duran's resurgence during the bout:

> **Bernstein**: Round 10, a big one for the Hands of Stone.
>
> **Clancy**: You know, the thing that amazes me is, I thought Duran at about the seventh or eighth round was really starting to show signs of weariness, but he came back and fought that last round like it was the first round.

The eleventh round was a continuation of Duran's resurgence. Midway through, Bernstein remarked:

> **Bernstein**: It hasn't been a bad round for Iran, we're halfway through. Who will win the second half?"

With Barkley's left eye starting to close, Duran delivered a pair of rock-hard right hands, and with about 30 seconds left in the round, he landed a 5-punch combination that sent Barkley down. The champion rose at the count of 7, but looked wobbly. Barkley spent the final seconds in retreat, and Duran could not find another knockdown punch. The bell sounded. Barkley walked around the ring apparently not sure where his corner was. He was wearing a smile, but he was hurt. The fans screamed their appreciation, with most feeling that Duran may have just cemented a historic upset win.

The bell for the twelfth and final round sounded. Barkley waited until the very last second to get up from his stool and walk out to touch gloves with Duran. The champion had to feel that that knockdown in the previous round may have put his title reign in jeopardy. Duran, no doubt, wanted to put an exclamation point on an incredible performance. It was an important final round for both fighters.

Barkley looked to have pulled himself back together as he came out and stood right in front of Duran firing good short punches. It was a close round to end things, sticking to the pattern of Barkley landing short hard shots, and Duran landing with sharp combinations. As the bell sounded to end the fight, Barkley immediately raised his hands and Duran stood with his hands down at his sides, bouncing and staring at Barkley. Duran's handlers immediately picked him up as he raised his hand in victory. On the other side of the ring, Barkley was walking around the ring with his hands raised.

The crowd was buzzing, and the electricity in the air flowed. The broadcasters made it very clear:

> **Clancy**: I wouldn't want to be a judge in this fight, Al.
>
> **Bernstein**: I wouldn't either. I would give the nod, personally, to Barkley. I thought he probably won more rounds, even with a two or three-point round by Duran. But it would be a very, very close call.

As both camps were waiting for the decision, the fans were in a celebratory mood. The two fighters hugged each other, sharing the mutual respect they had earned in the fight. It was genuine respect; it was clear that this would be an instant classic in the annals of boxing history. The ring was filled with people, a crush of humanity that wanted to be part of it all.

> **Bernstein**: Michael Buffer is in that mess somewhere; I don't know if he has the decision. We're waiting to find out.

The bell sounded for the decision to be announced. Michael Buffer was trying to tell the technicians that his microphone was not working. He spoke into it to demonstrate—no sound. The bell sounded again, and Buffer began his announcement, but again no sound in the arena. He looked with frustration over to the technicians. Apparently, the broadcast was picking up the mic signal, but the arena was not.

> **Buffer**: Ladies and gentlemen. Ladies and gentlemen. Ladies and gentlemen, your attention, please. Your attention, please.

Still no sound in the arena. He tapped the mic, but still no sound. He continued to tap the mic and say "test." With a crowd of thousands waiting to hear who got the decision in this remarkable fight, the pressure was really on Mr. Buffer. The fans waited impatiently as the arena techs scurried around trying to figure out where the sound went. As time went by, the fans in the arena were wondering what was taking so long to announce the decision. The tension built, on the fighters, their camps, and with most of the fans hoping against hope that they could erupt for Duran.

After nearly seven minutes from the sounding of the final bell, the decision was made to just go ahead and *yell* the decision out to the crowd. Calls for quiet were heard coming from somewhere in the middle of the sea of humanity that filled the ring.

Buffer began yelling out the decision to the crowd without the aid of electrified amplification:

> **Buffer**: Ladies and gentlemen, we have a split decision. Dave Brown scores the bout 116–113 for Barkley. Giuseppe Ferrari scores it 118–112 for Duran. Tommy Kaczmarek scores it 116–112 for the winner and *new* middleweight champion of the world...

You could not hear the name of Duran announced as the crowd cheered when they heard the word "new." Everyone realized that there was a new WBC middleweight king, and his name was Roberto Duran.

> **Gordon**: While Barkley was determined to retain his title, Duran wanted to win it even more. He was not to be denied. He battered the champion in the final few rounds, throwing punches with everything inside of himself. Although the decision was split, there was no doubt who the winner would be. It was one of the finest nights in the hall-of-fame career of the great Roberto Duran.

In the post-fight interview, Duran gave most of the credit to his conditioning, and added that Barkley was very strong. Barkley was gracious:

> **Barkley**: Well, I felt, I felt I was winning the fight. Roberto, Roberto is a legend, you know, so, quite naturally, I could figure that they'd do that. But, it was a good fight, you know, and the best man won, that's the way the judges called it, that's the way they see it. I've got to take my hat off to the man. He's a good man.

The fight earned the title of 1989's *Ring* Magazine Fight of the Year. And ring announcer Michael Buffer proved that you don't need electricity to announce a winner.

CHAPTER NINETEEN

Can You Hear Me Now?

Marvin Jones vs. Ramon Luis Nicolas

March 27, 2015
Arcadia, Florida

This eight-fight card held at the Turner Agri-Civic Center was televised on the Telemundo network and headlined by a WBO Latino super-flyweight championship bout. It was an explosive night of boxing, with five of the eight contests ending in the first round.

One of the night's undercard bouts featured a highly regarded Cuban prospect, Ramon Luis Nicolas, now living in and fighting out of Miami, who brought a pro record of two wins and one loss into his light-heavyweight match against Marvin "Papi Gallo" Jones, a Tennessee native living and fighting out of Puerto Rico. Jones brought a record of 2–4, and a reputation as a slugger. All of his six fights had ended in knockouts—one way or the other. Luis Nicolas was a world-ranked amateur for Cuba, and had a reported record of 350–21 in the unpaid ranks. His only loss as a professional came as a result of a disqualification against Dakota Dawson, in a fight he was dominating to that point, knocking Dawson down twice, but landing a shot to the shoulder of his opponent as he was on the canvas, which resulted in the disqualification loss. Nicolas was certainly the favorite in this match.

The bell rang. The two came out and touched gloves to start the match. Jones stepped back to get into his stance and an object fell out of his trunks. It was his cell phone. Referee Frank Santore halted the action and picked up the phone as he looked to Jones with a puzzled expression. Jones just put his hand out with the "I don't know" gesture. Telemundo's announcers Jessi Losada and Rene Giraldo had a good laugh with Losada saying (in Spanish), "I've seen it all now," as Jones respectfully bowed to the crowd at all four sides of the ring.

> **Sisneros**: A cell phone out of the trunks? What happened?
>
> **Jones**: The cell phone was a simple mistake that was made by my little brother while I was warming up.

They touched gloves again and went back to work. Both boxers seemed to be trying to establish their jab. Nicolas fought out of the southpaw stance and landed a few hard left hands in the exchanges. Jessi Losada just couldn't help himself as he laughed and interjected (in Spanish) that Jones may have to stop the fight during a round: "Excuse me, I have to take this call ... oh, it's my next fight!"

The fight moved along at a medium pace with Nicolas trying to land hard shots, and Jones looking calm and just missing with some sharp counter punches.

The timekeeper signaled for 10 seconds left in the round, and a second later Nicolas unleased a right-left combination that sent Jones down to the canvas. Santore began his count. At "5," the bell sounded to end the round, but the count continued as a fighter could not be saved by the bell in any round except the final. Jones sat alert and listened to Santore's count. He got up at "9," but Santore waved the fight off, giving the win to Nicolas as a technical knockout.

Jones was in disbelief. He showed his hands and appeared ready to continue the bout. Santore just shook his head "no" as the broadcast microphone picked up his comment to the disgusted fighter:

> **Santore**: You gotta get up before the count of 9. You were told that in the dressing room. The fight is over.

As the broadcast went to a commercial break, you could hear Santore continuing to explain things to Marvin Jones.

> **Sisneros**: Marvin, it looked like you were up before 10, but he stopped the fight anyway. What happened?
>
> **Jones**: Of course the ref and I would have different opinions on what happened that night.

It went down as an impressive win for the Cuban star who was still looking like a fighter to watch as this book went to press. He took a second loss three fights later, but it was another disqualification. Jones returned to Puerto Rico and fought nine months later, but was stopped in the second round.

Jones remains active helping his community in Puerto Rico:

> **Jones**: The most important part is the blessing that came after that night. with the mission of what I do with the youth and making people better through my gift and talents of boxing.

CHAPTER TWENTY

The Prophet of Doom

Marvin Hagler vs. Thomas Hearns Press Conference

April 1985
Los Angeles, California

Thomas Hearns' 1985 war with Marvin Hagler remains at the top of any fight fan's all-time favorite contests.

There was a massive build-up for what was one of the most anticipated fights of the decade. Marvin Hagler had not lost a fight in over nine years, and was considered an invincible fighting machine. Hearns was 40–1, with that lone loss coming in a *Ring* Magazine Fight of the Year against Sugar Ray Leonard. This was a matchup of two pound-for-pound kings.

There was a promotional campaign that helped to build up the already rabid anticipation for what would turn out to be another *Ring* Magazine Fight-of-the-Year. Neither Hagler nor Hearns were known as "talkers." They both earned their following by their performances in the ring. Like most really tough guys, they didn't *talk it*; they just *did it*. In the ring.

But for this promotional tour, they had to come out of their shells a bit, and do some trash talk. At one of the stops, in Los Angeles, Hagler kept it simple and stated that he was just going to knock Hearns out. Thomas "Hitman" Hearns then stepped up to the podium and made a clear prediction of what would happen, directing his statements to Hagler:

> **Hearns**: I predict three rounds. No more. No more, no less. But I can count to three, and I'm going to show you that I can count to three, and I can count a little bit past three. I'm going to count to four.

As Marvelous Marvin looked on with an amused expression, shaking his head a few times, Hearns continued:

> **Hearns**: I'm going to lead off, I'm going to start the fight off. I'm leading the fight off, I'm taking the fight to him. I'm going to start with combinations, 1, 2, 3. 1, 2, 3. 1, 2, 3 [tapping his fingers on the side of the podium with each number]. And when I finish with the 1, 2, 3's, I'm going to back off and add the 4. [He stepped back and demonstrated what he planned to do as he threw a volley of punches in the air.] Bam ... bam, bam, buh-bam... How can a man stand up for that? Boom. He's going to hit the floor [snapping his fingers and pointing to the floor].

Hagler just chuckled as Hearns finished with his vision of the future:

> **Hearns**: It's going to be a quick night. Buy your popcorn, your peanuts, and sit down, because if you don't, you're going to miss the fight!

Hearns was very entertaining in the way he presented his prediction. And he had the right number, but the wrong names. When the smoke cleared on April 15, 1985, it was Thomas Hearns that was laid out in round 3 of what was a glorious battle for the middleweight championship of the world.

For this fight, Marvelous Marvin Hagler was the true Prophet of Doom.

CHAPTER TWENTY-ONE

Oh Yeah, It Was a Punch!

Hugo Garay vs. Chris Henry

March 27, 2010
Monterrey, Nuevo Leon, Mexico

The main event for this card featured legendary champion Erik Morales in action against Jose Alfaro for a minor title.

It was an action-packed undercard, including one especially interesting 12-round light-heavyweight matchup between former NABF champion Chris "Hard Hitting" Henry (24–2, 19 KO) of Houston, Texas, and the former WBA world champion, Argentina's Hugo Garay (32–4, 17 KO).

Henry had climbed the light-heavyweight rankings ladder, and was hoping that a win over a former world champion would put him in line for a shot at a world title. In his previous fight, Henry defeated Shaun George by TKO to become qualified for the fight with Garay. The winner of this fight was to become the WBA's #1 ranked contender.

Garay had just lost his WBA title in his first defense by the thinnest of margins to Gabriel Campillo. Garay had tasted the title, and wanted to step over Henry to get it back.

Chris Henry's manager, Bob Spagnola, told me that this was not their first meeting:

> **Spagnola**: Chris had an amateur career, maybe 60 or 70 fights, he went to a major national tournament, and ends up going to an international tournament where he met Hugo Garay, who was a very accomplished amateur representing Argentina. So, they fought and he beat Chris, who was raw and didn't have that international skill set.

It was a very tense atmosphere as the boxers entered the ring. Serious faces all around. With referee Gerardo Aguilera giving the pre-fight instructions at ring center, the two glared at each other without a blink between them.

> **Spagnola**: Right from the beginning when we got there, he [Garay] was grabbing his crotch, and sticking out his tongue, talking all this mess in Spanish, calling Chris a "puto" and all of that.
>
> **Sisneros**: What did Chris think of that?
>
> **Spagnola**: We didn't say anything, but the minute he started that crap with Chris Henry ... Chris Henry was more than happy to *respond* to him. Because Chris was from the street and he wasn't about to back down to anybody. At the pre-fight press conference, Garay was talkin' all that, and the crowd was laughing. We didn't know what he was saying, but we knew it was not a compliment! Then at the weigh-in, it was held outdoors at a historic mall in Monterrey, and he was grabbing his self, and all of that crap. They got right up in each other's faces. So, we knew by the time they got in the ring, it was the same thing that had been going on for a week.

The Satellite broadcast team was "The Colonel" Bob Sheridan and Benny Ricardo. Sheridan got a kick out of the stare down, and the referee saying "buena suerte" (good luck). As the fighters walked back to their corners, he quipped:

> **Sheridan**: "Good luck." he says, and he has to push them away. The two fighters didn't want to leave the stare down.

Former champion Garay started fast, landing a short right hand and then throwing combinations at Henry who looked like he was trying to stop the attack by tying up Garay, but wasn't able to grab him, so he started firing back and made Garay back off. The two clinched, and the referee broke them. They were letting punches fly, both at medium range, and some inside fighting with Henry landing some clean body punches.

As Garay came inside, Henry calmly put his glove on the back of Garay's head and pushed down on him. It was a slick boxing move, but it still earned a warning from the referee.

With fifty-two seconds left in the round, Henry landed a short right hand that buckled the legs of Garay; as Garay tried to hold on, Henry pushed him away, and Garay fell flat on his back. As he laid there, stretched out, the referee began the count, but seeing no reaction from Garay, he waved the fight off. It was a knockout victory for Chris Henry.

> **Spagnola**: We knew it was a hard fight against a hard fighter. But when you look at that tape—that guy had Chris's left arm hooked—when a guy has your other arm hooked, it's really hard to land enough leverage to knock another man unconscious with that little room, and that little leverage. I didn't know at first what had happened.

The punch did not look that impressive, but it was a very short right hand high on the side of the head that put Garay down and out. The broadcasters didn't even catch it:

> **Sheridan**: See that right hand, that sneaky right hand in there ... then he pushes him down, I think that he's going to score that as a knockdown. Or is he? Yeah, he must have hit him with some shot, he's not getting up. The fight's all over!
>
> **Ricardo**: It's over! The back of his head hit the ground.
>
> **Sheridan**: The fight's all over. He knocked him out. What a shocking finish to this...
>
> **Ricardo**: Yeah, it was a right hand...
>
> **Sheridan**: I thought he pushed him over...
>
> **Ricardo**: Yeah, but it was originally the right hand.
>
> **Sheridan**: We gotta see the replay!

As soon as the referee waved the fight to a halt, Henry's trainer, Bobby Benton, came in and picked his man up as Henry began to celebrate the sudden knockout victory with raised arms.

Meanwhile, members of Garay's corner raced into the ring and began harassing referee Gerardo Aguilera. One man grabbed the ref by the arm, as the other pushed down on his neck as he was bending down to collect the scorecard from one of the judges. The whole scene turned ugly very fast.

Ricardo: They're trying to complain, right here, from the corner, and say ... no, no, but that wasn't a push! It was the right hand that did the initial damage.

Sheridan: Well, he told him to get up, if he was pushed down. And look at the corner of Garay. There's going to be some suspensions here!

The men continued to yell at and push the referee. It was starting to get too physical, when Henry's manager, Bob Spagnola, tried to step in and separate the men from their assault on the defenseless referee. The other members of Henry's team appeared to be trying to calm down the aggressors, and it worked. Things started to settle down, but Garay's cornermen continued to pace around the ring, obviously upset.

Louie Burke was working the corner of Henry that night:

Burke: We were trying to get between the ref and Garay's guys. They [Garay's corner people] weren't mad at *us*, we weren't sure what they were mad about, there was no bad blood between camps, or anything like that, but I felt like we should protect that referee.

Spagnola: Them Argentines came jumping into the ring, and honestly, I thought the police would be in right away, so I was just going to get in between these guys to protect that referee. But nobody did anything. If you notice on the tape, we had the referee in the corner, and I had David Rodriguez standing next to him. These guys were running all around acting crazy, but I knew eventually, they would realize... Garay doesn't *want* to get up!

While the scene was playing out in the ring, the broadcasters were reviewing the slow-motion video, trying to figure out exactly what happened:

Sheridan: Let's see...

Ricardo: There's the right hand...

Sheridan: *Oh, no!* It's a right hand!

Ricardo: And now watch... That's a great shot by our camera people. You're going to see the right hand.

> **Sheridan**: Yeah, he got him with a good right hand. I want to see the finish here.
>
> **Ricardo**: There was a right hand, and then the push. He never made a motion to get up. There's the right hand.
>
> **Sheridan**: Yeah, the right hand, and he pushed him down. Lennox Lewis made a career out of doing that.

The slow-motion video clearly showed a hard right hand landing high on the left side of Garay's head, causing the leg to buckle, and then as Garay tried to hold, Henry pushed him off and he went down, lying still and appearing to be knocked out.

The satellite broadcasters were able to listen in as referee Gerardo Aguilera was being asked by the Mexican Televisa network broadcaster about what just happened. Benny Ricardo translated for the US audience:

> **Ricardo**: Let's see what the ref here has to say... He said he [Garay] abandoned the fight. He did not want to get up. So if he doesn't want to get up, I gotta call off the fight.

It was a wild scene. It went down as a technical knockout at 2:20 of the first round. Bob Sheridan wrapped it up nicely:

> **Sheridan**: So a little bit of controversy, but not that much. After all, Chris Henry knocked him out.

Bob Spagnola said he left the arena not really knowing what had actually happened:

> **Spagnola**: Of course, I didn't know at first ... I didn't know at first what had happened. Literally after the fight, we went across the street to an Applebee's. Here we were in Monterrey, Mexico, at an Applebee's. The arena was a beautiful place, and they had a Jumbotron, but we couldn't see what had happened. Then we saw it on the slo-mo afterwards.

To make matters worse, the US contingent didn't even get paid for their services:

> **Spagnola**: Afterwards, we didn't get paid. David [Rodriguez] didn't get paid, and Chris didn't get paid. Two years later, I had to file a lawsuit, and we still haven't got paid!

Garay had a busy year and a half after this fight. He fought three more times, including a move up in weight to challenge for the WBO cruiserweight championship.

Chris Henry became ranked #1 by the WBA, but he would only fight once more, scoring a first-round knockout in Southaven, Mississippi. In August 2015, he was shot and killed in the parking lot of a Houston convenience store.

CHAPTER TWENTY-TWO

Unwanted Exposure

Rafael Limon vs. Sharmba Mitchell

March 8, 1990
Atlantic City, New Jersey

At the Trump Plaza Hotel's Imperial ballroom, 36-year-old Rafael "Bazooka" Limon, a man with 38 knockout wins, a veteran of over 70 pro fights, a former 2-time WBC world junior lightweight champion and former NABF champion, faced an undefeated rising 19-year-old prospect named Sharmba Mitchell, who was 13–0, with 6 knockout wins. If there ever was a "crossroads" bout, this was it. As broadcaster Al Albert mentioned, Mitchell was two years old when Limon made his professional boxing debut.

The bout was scheduled for eight rounds in the junior welterweight division. It was the power and experience of Limon against the speed and boxing of Mitchell. The pre-fight instructions were a bit unusual; instead of the usual stare down, Mitchell was more conventional in his demeanor, looking very serious as he listened to the referee's instructions. Limon listened with a big smile on his face. The USA network's Al Albert remarked:

> **Albert**: Well, uh, Bazooka Limon, happy to see Sharmba Mitchell. Not exactly a stare down. Very congenial was Bazooka.

As the opening round progressed, it was clear who the speed merchant was in this bout. Limon stuck his chin out at Mitchell, and was rewarded with a lightning-quick 1-2 combination, nothing damaging, but scoring blows. Mitchell fought a smart fight by not being available for the counters from Limon.

The second round saw Limon resort to more antics as he began holding his hands behind his back, daring Mitchell to hit him. Sharmba stayed under control, and continued pecking away. Limon made the "come here" motion while lying on the ropes, and Mitchell obliged with plenty of punches landed.

The two southpaws continued the battle in round 3 with Mitchell doing plenty of scoring, and Limon making plenty of gestures but not much scoring. With 30 seconds to go in the round, referee Paul Venti stopped the action to warn Limon not to hold on to the ropes.

Mitchell started the fourth round landing a huge left hand that turned the head of Limon, sending a spray of water from his hair. The difference in hand speed was obvious. Like a Ferrari against a Prius, Mitchell landed at will.

Limon began standing up between rounds rather than sitting on his stool in the corner. Venti went over and told him to stop hitting with an open glove.

In the fifth round, Limon seemed hesitant to launch punches as he was countered every time. Midway through the round, Limon backed up into a corner, and in a clinch, he reached down and appeared to be trying to pull down the trunks of his opponent with one hand. Mitchell backed away, and Limon followed him. Again engaging him in a clinch, he bent down, reached around with both gloves, and pulled down Mitchell's trunks. The referee jumped in and made the motion for the two fighters to re-engage, but Limon pointed at Mitchell's situation, and Venti realized that Mitchell would need some help adjusting his trunks as he stood there with his "tighty whities" and protective cup belt exposed. As the referee pulled up the trunks of Mitchell, Limon came over and patted Mitchell on the shoulder as if to apologize. The USA Broadcast team of Al Albert and Sean O'Grady had a good time with it:

> **O'Grady**: Sharmba Mitchell needed some more exposure, he got it!

In an exchange, Mitchell crouched and Limon began holding him down looking like he was "drumming" on the neck and back of his opponent. Venti was starting to get irritated with the antics of the former world champion, and yelled at him, "Cut it out! Cut it out!" as he pointed a finger in Limon's face.

Between the fifth and sixth rounds, Venti again went into the corner of Limon and made it very clear that the clowning had to stop. He threatened to stop the fight if Limon didn't get his act together.

The final three rounds saw Mitchell continue to torture Limon with punches that he could not find a way to avoid. In the sixth round, Mitchell landed a solid right hook, and Limon began to complain to the referee about a head butt, or thumb, but he did not receive much sympathy. A few seconds later Limon landed a kidney punch, and began holding Mitchell around the neck, bringing a stop in the action as Venti again pushed him back at the chest and yelled a few more times, "Cut it out! Cut it out, you understand me? Cut it out!" With just seconds left in the seventh round, Mitchell landed a powerful right hook that stunned Limon who immediately grabbed Mitchell around the legs. The bell rang, and Mitchell pushed on the head of Limon as he walked away.

The eighth and final round saw Limon trying to box from the outside, perhaps knowing that Mitchell was angry and would like nothing more than to knock him out. The 70-fight vet displayed his survival skills. Running, holding, clutching, grabbing, whatever it took to survive, that's what Bazooka Limon did. As pitiful as it was, the crowd seemed to be entertained in a weird way by the exhibition. But when the final bell sounded, the crowd gave a short chorus of booing. Boxing referee and historian Vic de Wysocki recalls:

> **Wysocki**: Paul Venti took the incident in stride and chose to simply caution Limon for "unsportsmanlike conduct," while the live television crowd booed their disapproval toward Limon's unprofessionalism. Mitchell ultimately went on to record a UD win.

Mitchell was glad to see this one come to an end. He earned a shut-out unanimous decision on scores of 80–72, 80–72, and 80–71. The fans gave Mitchell a loud ovation when the scores were announced, and Bazooka Limon was clapping for him with a big smile on his face. When ring announcer Ed Derian said, "Let's hear it one more time for Rafael "Bazooka" Limon!" the crowd unleashed a blast of boos.

> **Wysocki**: The moral of the story, as a referee you simply have to be prepared for "anything" happening inside the squared circle.

Bazooka Limon fought six more times over the next 4½ years, and even *tried to win* those bouts! He won two of them. Mitchell went on to claim the vacant NABF lightweight title, and later won the WBA junior welterweight title and the interim IBF junior welterweight title. He retired a bit over 16 years after this crazy night in a paid exhibition of sorts that allowed him to show *all* of his skills.

CHAPTER TWENTY-THREE

UFOs: They Exist in Boxing, Too!

Charles Anaya vs. Rudy Lovato

August 8, 1998
Albuquerque, New Mexico

Tonight was the long-awaited showdown between two local favorites. Rudy "Bad Boy" Lovato brought his 12–11, 4 KO record into the ring to face off against Charles "Poison" Anaya who was 5–1–1 with 3 KOs. Both were from Albuquerque, both had a huge following in town, and both were my friends. I was sitting at ringside with Henry Tafoya doing what was supposed to be the state-wide television broadcast, but it was never aired.

It was your classic crossroads battle. The 30-year-old Lovato came in with 23 pro fights. Despite Lovato's apparent advantage, it was an even matchup. Rudy started out as a world-class kick boxer and moved into boxing with less amateur boxing pedigree than his opponent. The 26-year-old Anaya had a good amateur boxing background, and came from a "boxing family": his father was one of New Mexico's top trainers, and his older brother Henry Jr. was a celebrated amateur boxer and had been a world-ranked professional contender during the late 1980s and early 1990s. Charles' nephew even went on to become a professional boxer.

There was some bad blood between the two camps, including an incident at an event five years earlier. It was nothing overly threatening, so the New Mexico State Athletic Commission approved the main event bout. Sandy Martinez-Pino, a commission member, recalls:

Martinez-Pino: As I work for the Albuquerque Police Department, I asked two good friends who were officers with APD to train and serve as deputy inspectors [for the state athletic commission]. My thought was I wanted to make sure someone in the position of authority was there to maintain the peace at the event.

Retired professional boxer Henry Anaya Jr. was working the corner for his little brother that night:

Anaya Jr.: There was some bad blood between the Lovato camp and our team from a prior fight between Rudy and one of our fighters, Anthony Chavez. That one turned into an all-out brawl at Roller West.

Rudy Lovato remembers his thinking going into the showdown fight:

Lovato: My thinking before the fight? It was "Okay, just win." The bad blood was, I think we were young and it was like, "My coach is better than yours," and wanting to be the best fighter in New Mexico, and some dumb stuff like that.

Fireworks were expected in the ring, but no one would have suspected the bout to end the way it did.

Martinez-Pino: Both of these boxers came from different barrios within Albuquerque and this fight was for more than a purse. It was for the winner being able to claim the distinction of having the best and baddest barrio. It was all about pride.

Lovato entered the ring dressed in black, with a black sparkling robe and black hat. He always relished the persona of being boxing's "bad boy." With hall-of-famer Bob Foster in his corner, he came in confident, all business.

Anaya had both his father and older brother in his corner. He was well-trained and ready for war.

The bout itself turned out to be more of a tactical battle than an all-out slugfest. Neither boxer was considered a real one-punch knockout threat. They went back and forth evenly, but by the second round, a little rabbit punching in the clinch brought a stern warning to both fighters from the referee.

In round 3, Lovato went down from an unintentional low blow, but quickly shook it off. Things heated up as Lovato scored with some big right hands, and began doing a "shimmy dance" in the middle of the ring, bringing the fans to their feet with their emotions starting to boil. The chant of "Poison! Poison! Poison!" arose between rounds 3 and 4 as Anaya's fans tried to fire their man up. It seemed to work, as he came out and landed some hard body shots that slowed Lovato's momentum. The referee gave frequent warnings for low blows and punching on the break to both fighters. It was down and dirty.

A series of tit-for-tat kidney and rabbit punches made the crowd erupt, with Lovato shooting a punch around the referee as he was breaking the two. Anaya retaliated, and they began throwing kicks with Nunez caught in the middle doing all he could to break the two. As the bell sounded, the ring was showered with debris; even a pair of sunglasses being thrown into the ring.

A group of state police officers made their presence known as they stood in each corner between rounds. Both corners tried to settle their fighters down; with so much at stake, they didn't want to have points taken, or worse, a disqualification loss. Nunez showed incredible patience by not deducting points or waving the fight off. With most of the fans on their feet throughout the entire battle, it felt like a smoking volcano just waiting to erupt. It did.

> **Martinez-Pino**: It was clear that the sold-out crowd was equally divided on who would support Lovato and who would support Anaya. From the minute the first bell rang there was holding and hitting, there were elbows thrown along with many other fouls including a low blow by Lovato. The ref was having a hard time controlling the bout no matter how he tried.

The two men settled back into a boxing match, relying on technique more than aggression. Henry Tafoya and I continued to do the broadcast at ringside. We felt a little relief as things started to calm down, but it wouldn't last. Tafoya was prophetic on the broadcast as he made the remark, "I have a feeling we haven't seen anything yet!" He was so right.

Martinez-Pino: I was on edge as I could feel the tensions rise during all rounds and unfortunately alcohol was being served even during the preliminary bouts which made matters worse. Then the unthinkable happened.

Round 8 was moving along evenly, good action, when Anaya dipped down and Lovato landed a rabbit punch. Referee Nunez called a halt to the action and ordered Lovato to the neutral corner while he tended to Anaya, making sure that he was able to continue. As Lovato stood in the corner waiting for the action to continue, another hail of debris was launched into the ring, including an object that turned out to be a half-filled Pepsi bottle that hit Lovato in the shoulder. He went down, covering his head with his gloved hands, not knowing what had just hit him and what might follow.

Lovato: I wasn't worried about the fight; I knew I had it. The Pepsi bottle was a surprise, the bottle tipped my nose, then things went crazy, but security did what they thought best. Great job on their behalf.

Sisneros: Rudy, didn't it hit you in the shoulder, too?

Lovato: Yeah, it tipped my nose and hit me in the shoulder. The shoulder took it good. It was a little more than half full.

All civility broke down in the near riot conditions as the state athletic commission officials struggled with the question of what to do. Lovato was looked at by the attending physician, and he and his team were escorted out of the ring, back to the locker room area. The state police filled the ring as announcer Mike Adams tried every trick in the book to calm the crowd down, including having Henry Anaya Jr. address the crowd and ask for calm, only to be met with loud profanity from someone in the crowd. Adams reminded the crowd that there were children present. Charles Anaya himself took the microphone and pleaded for calm. But it was too late; the fight was called by the state athletic commission.

Martinez-Pino: Chaos ensued and I looked to my left and to my right. Fights were breaking out everywhere

> and I was the only commissioner still at the table. The other commissioners in attendance had crawled under the ring and were nowhere to be found. My two officers were stellar in maintaining protection, especially for me. Certainly there wasn't enough security to deal with all the fighting fans, but I was kept safe. As the only commissioner still visible, I was handed the score cards so I was aware of who won this very close bout. I knew that half of this drunk crowd wasn't going to like the decision.

To avoid further violence, it was announced to the crowd that the fight was halted due to an injury suffered by Rudy Lovato, and the rounds fought would be scored, in private, with the decision announced the next day in the Albuquerque newspapers.

> **Lovato**: After they took me back to the dressing room when all the mayhem is going on, I knew I was going to win the fight on disqualification. Before we left, the commission did go back and told me that I had won on the disqualification and then the rest of the night I didn't worry about anything. We went out and partied as usual, you know how I was. The next morning, I wanted to see what was written in the paper and see if they had caught whoever threw the bottle.

> **Sisneros**: OK, but they scored the bout by score cards, and had you the winner. It officially went down as a technical decision win for you, 79–73, 79–75, and 77–75.

> **Lovato**: Oh, crap! I had always thought it was just a disqualification from what I was told. I'm going to have to look that up!

Those scores were reported and made official: with all three judges in agreement, the technical decision was unanimous in favor of Rudy Lovato.

> **Martinez-Pino**: I looked under the ring and asked the chairman of the commission how he wanted the winner announced with judges scores being read. His answer was, "You do whatever you want on the announcement." At that point Rick Wright, boxing writer for the *Albuquerque Journal*, came over and asked about the

> winner. I told him that because of the behavior of the crowd a winner would not be announced until Monday in the *Albuquerque Journal*. When the decision was announced *not* to announce a winner to the crowd in attendance, there was a lot of complaining and whining by fans of both boxers, but ultimately both sides left and I breathed a huge sigh of relief. My two officers escorted me out of the venue and walked me to my car. That night I did give Rick Wright the winner and the scores without judges' names being attached with the assurance that he would not print it until Monday's edition.

It was a night that anyone present will never forget. You would think that with all of the intense negative emotions swirling around these two fighters, it would be a lifelong feud. But no, the two actually became good friends away from the ring. They both expressed respect for each other to me after this encounter. I was surprised, but glad to hear it. I thought the world of both of them, and did not want this to remain a lifelong feud.

> **Anaya Jr.**: Long story short, we put our differences aside years ago and have been friends for a long time now—to the point that I think Rudy asked me to train or manage years ago, I don't even remember, exactly. And currently, he has been helping out my son Henry Anaya III with some training and helping get some pro fights lined up. I guess if things like that fight didn't happen we wouldn't have stories to tell or write about.

Sadly, "Poison" Anaya would not fight again. He died three years later. He was and remains one of the most beloved figures in the Albuquerque boxing community, and in October 2017 he was inducted into the New Mexico Boxing Hall of Fame.

Rudy Lovato would go on to fight for nine more years. He became renowned as one of boxing's "Minute Men," taking short-notice calls all over the country to fight, and competing in 41 more bouts before retiring from the ring. He now gives back to the community by training young boxers. Like Anaya, he is a beloved member of New Mexico boxing history.

CHAPTER TWENTY-FOUR

Wild Night in Oklahoma

John Jackson vs. Casey Ramos

April 23, 2011
Thackerville, Oklahoma

An event broadcast by Fox Sports at the WinStar Casino featured Detroit native John "Action" Jackson (15–2–1, 13 KO) set for eight rounds against the unbeaten Casey "The Wizard" Ramos (12–0, 4 KO) out of Austin, Texas. On paper, it certainly looked like an interesting matchup. Ramos was unbeaten, and was being looked at as an up-and-comer. Jackson had 13 knockouts in his 15 wins, and was coming off of a loss by technical decision in a challenge for the interim NABA junior lightweight title in his previous outing.

Boxing writer and historian Lee Groves noted the importance of this match to both fighters:

> **Groves**: Boxing is, was, and always will be a serious sport. So, in that vein, when it decides to get weird, it gets *seriously* weird. Such was the case in this match between Casey Ramos and John Jackson. This was a crossroads match in which Ramos sought to extend his undefeated record while Jackson was seeking to rebound from a shaky two-fight stretch in which he drew with Willshaun Boxley and suffered a technical decision loss to Eusebio Osejo in Nicaragua, the first (and only) time he would fight outside the US. The scuttlebutt going in was that both were skilled fighters but that Ramos had faced the better opposition.

As round 1 began, Jackson made full use his height and reach advantage, while Ramos was steady and throwing hard punches at his mobile opponent. The fight pattern was obvious: Jackson using movement and working behind his jab, Ramos using timing and counter punching. With about 48 seconds to go in the round, Jackson tied Ramos up, grabbing him around the waist. Referee Gary Ritter called for them to break, and as Jackson stepped back with his hands down, Ramos launched a power-packed right hand that sent Jackson crashing to the canvas. The referee immediately scolded Ramos for his actions, waved his arms that it was not a knockdown, called for time, and ordered Ramos to the neutral corner. He then called for the ring doctor to enter and examine Jackson. Jackson rose up, but looked shaky. His mouthpiece fell out. His corner yelled at him to stay down and take the full time he needed to recover. He went to one knee as he awaited instructions from the referee and ring doctor. After the doctor questioned him and consulted with the referee, he was directed into the red corner, where the doctor continued to talk to him and have him follow his finger with his eyes. Jackson was then directed to his own corner to have his mouthpiece replaced. After nearly three minutes, the fight continued. Jackson appeared fully recovered as he aggressively pursued Ramos, who looked like he was eager to finish the fight, but the bell soon sounded. There was no point deduction, but a strict warning was issued to Ramos for the foul.

The second round opened with Jackson looking fully recovered, and Ramos continuing to put on the power-punching pressure. One minute into the round, the referee called for a break, and again, Ramos unleashed. This time it was a left hand that connected. Jackson was nailed solidly, but he didn't go down. Ritter wasted no time in calling for a time out. He deducted one point from Ramos for hitting on the break. As he grabbed the right hand of Ramos and turned to each of the three judges telling them clearly, "1 point for hitting on the break!" Ramos tried to plead his case with the referee, but Ritter was not going to allow his voice commands to be ignored. He checked with Jackson once more, to make sure that he was fine to continue, and then Jackson came out swinging. The round finished with Ramos using hard counter punches and body punches to keep Jackson on the move and looking for angles to attack.

Jackson started the third round fast, perhaps trying to build on that point deduction in round 2. He scored with a quick, sharp right hand that brought a little noise from the crowd, but for most of the round it looked like Ramos just had more power, and was landing some stinging body shots. The final half of the round saw Ramos press the attack. Jackson wasn't running, but he *was* retreating. The final seconds saw Ramos land some hard shots to the head. It was a solid round in favor of Ramos.

Round 4 saw more of the same, as Ramos began attacking more than countering. With half of the round gone, Ramos landed a low left hand that drew a warning from the ref to "keep 'em up." The two exchanged combinations to the body, but it was clearly Ramos' attack that was more damaging. With 30 seconds left, Ramos landed a solid three-punch combination that stung Jackson, followed by a hard right hand to the body that brought a smile to the face of Jackson who stuck his tongue out. Ramos then landed a solid right to the chin that froze Jackson, and then another right that sent him crashing into the ropes and down on to the second rope (of four) from the top. The rope came unhooked from the ring post, which took Jackson down to the second rope from the bottom that held him up as he was bent over, clearly hurt from the two right hands he had just absorbed. The referee correctly ruled that the ropes were holding him up, and it was a knockdown. Jackson slowly stood up and took the mandatory 8-count from the referee. He turned and walked slowly and wobbly to his corner, as the mouthpiece fell out of his mouth while the referee finished his count. The referee felt that he had spit out the mouthpiece on purpose, and deducted one point for that action.

The action was halted while a maintenance crew went to work trying to fix the ropes. The two fighters were allowed to wait in their respective corners. Ramos stood and fidgeted back and forth on his feet, while Jackson chose to be seated on his stool. After nearly a 12-minute delay, the problem was fixed and the bout was allowed to start with an immediate ringing of the bell to finally and officially end the round.

It was a bad one for John Jackson: he had lost the round, gotten knocked down, and had a point deducted. Fox Sports broadcaster Rich Marotta asked:

Marotta: What else can happen here on the plains of Oklahoma? Helicopter, I don't know?

Round 5 started with the two fighters well rested after the long break. Even though he was way down on the score cards, Jackson came out boxing. He moved around the ring, circling and trying to sneak in punches from long range, but it was still Ramos landing the blows. At the end of the round, Jackson tied Ramos up, and as he voluntarily backed away with his hands down, Jackson was caught with a short left hand that got his attention. The bell rang, and Jackson looked at the referee with a palms-up gesture, but there was no command to stop.

Groves: If there was a broadcast team that was perfectly suited to document this situation, it was Barry Tompkins and Rich Marotta. While they are polished professionals who know the ins and outs of the sport, they also share an appreciation for the absurd. Their breezy delivery was perfect for that situation.

The Fox Sports team commented:

Tompkins: So we come to round 6 of this 8-round fight. Ramos gotta pick it up right where he left off after that *long* break.

Marotta: Yeah, there was another little moment right at the end of the round. I think Jackson thought they were breaking apart after they were in close, and he relaxed again and Ramos hit him, but there was not a break from a clinch. You've gotta keep your hands up. You've gotta protect yourself at all times, and not be expecting the other guy to stop punching just because you put your hands down and start walking away.

Tompkins: First rule of boxing.

Marotta: And he complained to the referee, but there was no clinch and break called.

Lee Groves gives referee Gary Ritter high marks on his performance that crazy night:

Groves: Because the incident occurred near the end of the round, Ritter ruled that once the rope had been repaired, he would declare the round over, then give the fighters an additional one-minute break, ostensibly to restore the regular rhythm of the fight. Despite all the bizarre circumstances, Ritter was a rock of stability throughout.

Round 6 went by without any more incidents, although with 30 seconds to go, Jackson again tied up with Ramos, and then as he voluntarily backed away got partially caught with a right hand. He again made a gesture of frustration, and again the Fox Sports team remarked on it:

> **Tompkins**: Right hand again, he thinks it's on the break.
>
> **Marotta**: It's not.
>
> **Tompkins**: It was not this time, you're right.
>
> **Marotta**: Same thing that occurred at the end of the last round. He's complaining about it, but they're not in a clinch.

The final two rounds passed with pretty much the same pattern going to the end. Jackson tried to stick and move around the ring, but continued to get caught with hard power punches from Casey Ramos.

Between the seventh and eighth rounds, Jackson's trainer told him: "We need this round like a junkie needs a fix!"

> **Marotta**: If this fight goes the distance, the break of the rope will have been the biggest break for John Jackson.
>
> **Tompkins**: Yeah, he was done, I think.

In the final round, Ramos was in command. He did seem to be slowing down, and why not? He had thrown a lot of hard punches, and was in command throughout the fight against an opponent that made himself a difficult target. He was slowing down, but still effective.

> **Groves**: Due to the long break, this eight-round fight was really two four-rounders with a 15-minute break in between. Ramos dominated both halves, and, thankfully, rounds five through eight were as conventional as the first four rounds were unconventional.

There was not much suspense as the scores were read by ring announcer Lupe Contreras. With all of the chaos witnessed by the judges, they all had it the same.

Groves: When the judges' scorecards were tallied, it was interesting to note that all three jurists scored the fight identically: 79–70 for Ramos.

As the broadcast went to break, Marotta remarked:

Marotta: Well, perhaps the most impressive win of Casey Ramos' career. He runs his record now to 13 and 0, in a strange fight, one that had point deductions from both fighters, a knockdown that wasn't, a broken rope that resulted in a delay, here, of close to 15 minutes during the fifth round, but nonetheless, Casey Ramos emerges with the victory.

Boxing historian Lee Groves wraps it up:

Groves: One could say that Ramos was denied a knockout victory not once, but twice. The first opportunity was squandered by Ramos himself because of his fouling, but the second chance was lost because of the fates. Ramos may have been nicknamed "The Wizard," but in this fight something, or someone, else was casting the spells.

As of this writing, both fighters are still active.

CHAPTER TWENTY-FIVE

Surprise Visit

Christy Martin vs. Lucia Rijker Incident

March 1, 2000
Los Angeles, California

Just days before Christy Martin was to step into the ring against New York's Belinda Laracuente, there was a public workout for fans of Martin, who at the time was considered one of boxing's top women fighters, to see the popular boxer as she wound down her training regimen for the upcoming fight.

Lucia Rijker was 14–0 with 13 knockouts. She was considered the most threatening woman in boxing, and she was coming up fast. She also wanted to get Martin into the ring.

That bout was much talked about, but never got made. Rijker thought she would remind the boxing world that she was clamoring for a chance to fight Martin, nicknamed "The Coal Miner's Daughter."

Only the aftermath of this brief encounter was caught on videotape. Martin claimed that she was doing an interview when Rijker came up and punched her in the face as she turned away. Some of the people present said that it was Martin who started it by pushing Rijker.

The video aired on Showtime's broadcast before Rijker's fight with Laracuente. It showed a chaotic scene with people trying to keep the two apart. Rijker was on the ground with a man holding her down by the throat, and Martin was being held back by several gentlemen.

Rijker got to her feet, very calmly and quietly saying, "C'mon, c'mon," while making a gesture with one hand for Martin to approach her. Martin was enraged and yelling that

Rijker had just sucker-punched her. Rijker was escorted out of the building, and calm was restored.

> **Martin**: If you really are a true fighter, you're not going to come up and try to steal on somebody three or four days before they fight. You don't do that.

As Martin spoke, promoter Don King chimed in with: "Unprofessional! Unprofessional!"

> **Martin**: And then the fight can be made. I've been asking for the fight, she didn't want it. She says she needs to fight a man, that no woman will fight her. But every time she has a woman's fight scheduled, she pulls out.

Showtime's Steve Albert shared:

> **Albert**: While Christy said Lucia started it, bystanders tell us that Christy started it by shoving Lucia. In any case, the scuffle ensued. Cameras started rolling after the punch. Martin ruptured the tendons in two fingers in her right hand and injured an ankle in the melee. But she said she was okay for tonight. It nearly put tonight's fight in jeopardy, affecting two fighters. Rijker was frustrated over inability to get a real fight with Christy. Very unfortunate episode, indeed.

Despite the incident, Martin won a very close majority decision over Laracuente.

Martin's career went on for 12 more years, with 16 more fights. She went 10–5–1 down that stretch. Rijker did not fight for the rest of 2000, or all of 2001. She had one fight a year for 2002, 2003, and her final fight in 2004. She won them all and retired from the game with a perfect 17–0 record. Perhaps Rijker lost interest in a fight with Martin after Christy's fourth round TKO loss to Laila Ali, or just got tired of chasing after that dream fight with Christy Martin.

Former professional boxer and current WIBA president Ryan "Kid Smooth" Wissow lamented:

> **Wissow**: I was looking forward for it [the "super fight'] to happen and I was bummed about it getting cancelled.

The two never met in what could have been a very interesting meeting. Or should I say, the two never met ... in the ring.

CHAPTER TWENTY-SIX

The Bonus Round

Ernest Mateen vs. Rich LaMontagne

May 2, 2003
Mashantucket, Connecticut

Despite this event being officially announced as an ESPN2 *Friday Night Fights* broadcast, it was shown on tape delay the next night as a result of the NBA playoffs. The semi-main event was a cruiserweight bout scheduled for 10 rounds between 36-year-old Ernest "M-16" Mateen, a New York native, fighting out of West Palm Beach, Florida, and 33-year-old Richie "The Mountain" LaMontagne.

Both fighters were well-respected, ranked contenders. Mateen was older and perhaps on the downside of his career, but had some big names on his record. He had plenty left, as was proven in his previous fight, winning the USBO cruiserweight title via clear technical decision against Uriah Grant. LaMontagne may not have had the names on his ledger, but he was younger, had the better record, and was coming off of a knockout win over former US Olympian Michael Bennet in his previous fight. Everything in their records pointed to an entertaining bout—including Mateen's attitude:

> **LaMontagne**: He was a dirty talker. A street-punk kind of guy. He was bad mouthing me and all that.

The bout started with both boxers working their jabs. While clinching, Mateen fired a couple of right hands to the kidney of LaMontagne, bringing a warning from referee Ken Ezzo.

They were exchanging pretty evenly in the second round when, with 1:09 left, Mateen slammed home a right hand that shook LaMontagne. In the last few seconds of the round, the two were rough housing in a clinch, and referee Ezzo stopped the action to warn them both to keep it clean. The bell rang, and it looked like a good round for Mateen.

"M-16" Mateen started the third round with another smashing right hand that sent LaMontagne back to the ropes. He continued the busy attack, and even though many of the punches were blocked and slipped by LaMontagne, plenty were getting through—certainly enough to win another round.

Round 4 started with the ESPN2 broadcast team of Bob Papa and Teddy Atlas discussing Mateen's apparent lead in the fight:

> **Papa**: Teddy, Goody Petronelli, the longtime trainer in the corner of Rich LaMontagne said, "Hey, you've got to get busier. You've lost all three rounds."
>
> **Atlas**: I almost agree with him. I give LaMontagne the first round. He's trying to wake up his fighter, who definitely is not having his way with the very gutsy, hungry, experienced Mateen. Mateen is not in there with a big puncher tonight. He doesn't have that disadvantage where his chin's going to be exposed or where he's going to pay the final price if he gets caught with one shot. His experience, his heart, his right-hand power can come into play, and it has.

Meanwhile, the fight pattern continued with Mateen controlling the center of the ring, and LaMontagne moving around the outside looking for effective angles to get his shots in. Things suddenly went off-script when LaMontagne landed a right cross that connected to the chin of Mateen, sending him down to his back. He was up at the count of seven, but looked wobbly and a little stunned. The referee asked him if he was okay and made Mateen walk toward him. Satisfied, he allowed the bout to continue. LaMontagne looked for some finishing shots, but Mateen kept bulling his way forward, trying to stay out of the range to get caught clean with another bomb. With one minute left in the round, Mateen charged forward and, while the referee was breaking the two fighters, his mouthpiece came out, earning him a few more seconds to regroup. The broadcasters suspected it was intentional:

Atlas: Valuable break, very important break for Mateen.

Papa: I think he conveniently lost that in that tie-up. Little more time.

The corner for Mateen washed out the mouthpiece and replaced it. The action resumed. Mateen was holding and the referee ordered a break. As LaMontagne did as instructed and stepped back, Mateen fired a short left hand that didn't land on LaMontagne, but did catch the side of the head of the referee, who deducted one point. Between the knockdown and the point, it was a disastrous round for Mateen.

As the bell rang to start round 5, time was called as the ring physician came in for a quick look at Mateen. He gave the "OK" and the action started. The original pattern of the fight resumed, with Mateen more or less stationary in the middle of the ring and LaMontagne moving around the outside. Mateen was caught with a stiff right hand that brought a cheer from the crowd.

The pattern of styles looked the same, but the demeanor of the two combatants had changed. Mateen now looked shaky and uncertain, while LaMontagne had gained an aura of confidence. Just a little more than halfway through the round, the referee called for a time-out in the bout due to an accidental clash of heads, and had the doctor come in to look at Mateen again. He had a pretty bad cut over his left eye, but the doctor felt he was fine and so the round continued. Mateen was complaining about something, and with 50 seconds left in the round the referee had enough and ordered Mateen to "Shut up, and let's go!" As time wound down, Mateen looked frustrated. The bell sounded and the two went to their corners.

Between rounds, the doctor came in to check on Mateen. The ESPN microphone picked up referee Ken Ezzo very clearly state: "No, no, if he's seeing double, that's it!" He then turned around and waved his hands in the air: The fight was over.

LaMontagne came over to speak with Mateen, but it didn't go so well: LaMontagne shrugged his shoulders and stepped back with his hands up, and things unraveled from there.

LaMontagne: I just went over to him to say, "Hey, man, good fight, don't feel bad about the ending, it was a tough fight." He started saying, You head-butted me, you m***er f***er!" I said "What?" "You head-butted me!" He just kept on, so I said, "Put your hands up, let's go!" He didn't do anything until the ref came over there and then as soon as the ref came over, he started.

In an instant it all broke loose. The referee tried to hold one of Mateen's cornermen in place when Mateen lashed out with a swatting right hand which was like a signal to everyone to begin brawling. That's when the crowd was treated to a "bonus round." Everyone in the ring took the cue to begin swinging and grabbing each other. Uniformed officers and men in suits swarmed the ring to regain control of the situation.

Papa: Oh! Mateen with a sucker punch. And we have a melee here at Foxwoods. There's more fighting after the bell than in the fight.

Atlas: Mateen said something to LaMontagne as they came close. LaMontagne said, "C'mon, you wanna go?"

LaMontagne took exception to a sucker punch thrown by Mateen, and tried to dive at him, but with everyone holding everyone else, it was hard to get through. It was a frantic scene that just flared up and exploded into a burst of aggression. Security did a good job of holding everyone in place, and things started to cool off just as quickly as it had started.

When LaMontagne realized that things were settling down, he went over to the corner and stood on the ropes holding his hands up, getting a huge cheer from the supportive crowd. Mateen and his team exited the ring and headed for the locker room area. Papa and Atlas continued to analyze the situation while reviewing slow-motion replay:

Papa: They're both complaining about head butts, you hit me in my eye, you hit me in my eye. LaMontagne says you, "Wanna keep fighting?"

Atlas: And see that was wrong right there. Up to that point it was all talk. It was bravado. You can see it was two guys that were feisty. But then, that sneak sucker punch over the shoulder by Mateen. That was something that was uncalled for.

Papa: Right, but you know what, Teddy? LaMontagne has some of the blame here, too. Because they were both talking a little trash about the head butt and LaMontagne is the one who backed up and got into "you want to keep this fight going." Right? We just saw that right there. LaMontagne went into his fight pose.

Atlas: You're right. You're absolutely right about that, but once the people had gotten in between, the punch was thrown over the shoulder of a couple of guys by Mateen.

The fight went down as a technical knockout win for Richie LaMontagne. The ESPN crew concluded that there was plenty of blame to go around for the out-of-control ending to the bout.

I asked LaMontagne if he thought the ESPN broadcasters had gotten it right:

LaMontagne: It takes two to tango. But, he was more punkish about it. I'm a clean fighter, I'm clean about it. He head butted me, but his cut came from a right hand.

LaMontagne went on to fight four more times, with his final bout an unsuccessful challenge for the WBU cruiserweight title against Enzo Maccarinelli in England a little less than two years later. When I talked to him in February of 2017, he was still ready to get back to the ring:

LaMontagne: I'm in great shape, and looking to get back in the ring. I stay in shape and I spar with these 25-year-old guys. I can still do it.

Sisneros: Rich, how old are you?

LaMontagne: I'm 45. I'm in great shape. I stay busy in the gym.

Sisneros: I guess at your age, that's what makes it hard to get a fight?

LaMontagne: Yeah, they look at your age, but look at George Foreman, he was like 50 when he fought his last fight, y'know? I can still do it.

Ernest Mateen would fight five more times, with his final bout in June of 2006, a 10-round decision win over Terry Porter. Mateen died in 2012, at the age of 46, shot to death by his wife. It was ruled self-defense.

CHAPTER TWENTY-SEVEN

Late Night Shopping

Mitch Green vs. Mike Tyson Street Brawl

August 23, 1988
Harlem, New York

In August of 1988, Mitch "Blood" Green got his rematch with Mike Tyson, but it was not in the ring.

Tyson and Green met in May of 1986 at Madison Square Garden in New York. Tyson was an undefeated phenom on his way up at that time. Green was a ranked contender whose only loss was to Trevor Berbick in a very close majority decision for the USBA heavyweight title belt. In their first encounter, Tyson won a lopsided unanimous decision over 10 rounds.

Green spent two years trying to get a rematch with Tyson, who had become the biggest draw in boxing as the undisputed heavyweight champion of the world.

As Tyson went in to a specialty clothing store called Dapper Dan's Boutique in the wee hours of the morning, he was approached by Green who began airing some of his grievances with the champ. New York native and boxing historian Robert Silva recalls the infamous incident:

> **Silva**: I remember that morning after the Tyson-Green street fight occurred. I was walking out my apartment in the MillBrook housing projects located in the nefarious South Bronx. At the time I was 20 years old and a few weeks away from returning to college. Everyone in my neighborhood knew me and my father as the reigning boxing experts of the South Bronx. I was stopped by a couple of drug dealers who revealed to me that Tyson and Green had gotten into an altercation outside of

> Dapper Dan's store in Harlem. Back then, Dapper Dan was the man who designed all the major drug dealers, athletes, and entertainer's suits. Tyson and legendary NYC and St John's basketball star Walter Berry were leaving the store when Green approached Tyson, claiming that Tyson and Don King owed him money from their MSG fight two years prior.

It depends on who you get the story from as to what actually happened that morning. Tyson said that Green approached him:

> **Tyson**: I was nervous, 'cause, y'know, I hadn't had a fight, like a street fight, in seven years. I was scared, and I was getting paranoid 'cause he was so close, he kept getting close to me. So, I just defended myself.

When asked who threw the first punch, Green remembered it differently:

> **Green**: He did. He sucker-punched me. 'Cause he was with his friends. Y'know, when he hit me, I didn't have a chance to get to him like I wanted to, because everybody was like pulling me, y'know, holding me, like so he could get away from me. So he could get away. And he, like, he ran from me, but I was trying to get to him, y'know. And, like I said, I wanted to take a little more hands, you know, at that moment, you know, I was serious. I was outraged. I wanted to go off.

The store's night manager, Damon Abramson, witnessed the whole thing:

> **Abramson**: Mitch kept ranting and raving, and Mike stood up because he had made contact. Mike said, "Look, do not play me close," in other words, back off, don't get that close to me. So then Mitch grabbed his shirt, and apparently went for his pocket because his wallet fell out. Mitch Green threw the first blow. Now, Mike Tyson did what any man, resident of the United States... Green punched him in the chest—right around this area right here. And, I mean, Mike Tyson is Mike Tyson, he's not gonna have that from anyone.

Abramson described Tyson beating on Green who was on his back after being taken down by Tyson and the two were going at it. It must have been some pretty hard action. Tyson ended up suffering a fractured right hand which he had in a cast during a news conference about the incident. Green's eye was swollen shut, and stitches were needed to close a cut on the bridge of the nose.

> **Silva**: Green then ripped Tyson's shirt, causing Tyson to land one of the greatest right crosses of his career, instantly closing Green's left eye and also breaking Tyson's right hand. Green, in his tomfoolery, is lucky Tyson didn't kill him, as Mike was going through a period in his life that was both mentally and emotionally stressful for him. His marriage to Robin Givens and the death of mentor Jimmy Jacobs, as well as the devilish machinations of Don King had the then 22-year-old baddest man on the planet in emotional turmoil.

If this was all a ploy to get a big money fight with Mike Tyson, it didn't work. The two never had a rematch. Green made a bit of a comeback about 4½ years after this incident. He went 3–4 with 1 no-contest before hanging up his gloves in 2005. Tyson continued as the biggest draw in professional boxing and went on to secure his place in boxing immortality, but it was a hard road to get there. He, like Green, fought his final bout in 2005.

> **Silva**: A few months later, Tyson attempted suicide by wrapping his car around a pole. That morning, after hearing what happened, I felt empathy for Tyson, and my father felt it was only a matter of time before Tyson would implode. History shows my father was correct in his assessment.

Mike now uses this incident as part of the material for his one-man stand-up stage routine.

CHAPTER TWENTY-EIGHT

The Sucker Punch

James Butler vs. Richard Grant II

November 23, 2001
New York, New York

This day will not be forgotten by those in attendance at the Roseland Ballroom in New York City, or by the ESPN2 broadcast audience, who witnessed one of the most shocking moments in boxing history.

James "The Harlem Hammer" Butler stepped into the ring in hopes of avenging his first of only two career losses in a rematch with fellow contender Richard "The Alien" Grant.

Butler had just lost a twelve-round decision to undefeated IBF super-middleweight champion Sven Ottke in a bid for the title 2½ months earlier. His 18–2, 12 KO record made James Butler the certain favorite over 13–8, 2 KO Richard Grant, even though Grant held a decision win over Butler in a four-round bout very early in their careers. Boxing historian Vernon Gravely was expecting a good technical boxing match:

> **Gravely**: It was a classic case of boxer (Grant) versus puncher (Butler). Grant had bested Butler once before, a four-round decision victory in 1997, in the third professional outing for each fighter.

As referee Mike Ortega asked both boxers to touch gloves after being given the pre-fight instructions at center ring, an animated Butler, wearing trunks with "Butler" written across the front waist band, "9-11" on one leg, and an American flag on the other, was jumping around and moving side-to-side. He swung and missed with a slap at the outstretched glove of Grant. The referee ordered them again to "touch-em-up" and

Butler reluctantly slapped away the glove of the blond Grant. This may have been a sign of the mood that Butler was in.

Grant had apparently studied well as he had a great fight plan to control the power in the hands of Butler. With steady movement and great timing, Grant spent the 10 rounds sticking and moving from the outside, frustrating Butler, who was loading up and hoping to catch his tricky opponent somewhere along the way. It never happened.

As the rounds went by, Grant stayed focused and continued to frustrate his powerful opponent. The few punches Butler threw were loaded with knockout juice, but not connecting. By round 7, Grant became totally confident and began dropping his hands, sticking his jaw out and daring Butler to flail away in hopes of landing the one punch that would change things. James Butler was intent on a sudden ending. Not much jabbing, no body punching, no feints, just bombs.

By the ninth round, Butler's left eye began swelling, and he was showing a little wear and tear from the punches landed by his light hitting, but busier opponent. ESPN2's broadcast duo of Teddy Atlas and Bob Papa had Grant far out in front, and it looked like Butler's only hope was to score a knockout, or at the least several knockdowns before the final bell.

In the tenth and final round, Butler's frustration began to show as he received a warning from Ortega for hitting on the break. Ortega could be heard telling Grant, "Don't retaliate," and "Keep it clean, keep it clean." A great sentiment, if only it had been heeded after the bout was over. Grant also received a warning from the ref for holding, a strategic tactic that had served him well throughout the bout as he tied up his powerful opponent's attempts at counter punches. The final 40 seconds of the bout ticked away with Butler chasing Grant all over the ring, firing knockout punch after knockout punch that missed his moving target. With just a few seconds left in the fight, Butler landed a pair of left hands that shook Grant, but time ran out before he could follow up. The bell sounded to end the bout and the two fighters returned to their corners, Grant with hands raised feeling confident of victory, Butler walking with a more serious gait, but still hoping to get the decision based mostly on his aggressive movement.

> **Gravely**: Truthfully, it wasn't a very exciting fight. It wasn't boring, by any means, but the fact is, Richard Grant did what he had to do to win, and James Butler seemed to be content to let Grant lead, which cost him the fight. And, if not for the incident that immediately followed Michael Buffer's announcement of the decision, it probably would have been a quickly forgotten one.

Ring announcer Michael Buffer read off the score cards of 96–94, 97–93, and 97–93, all in favor of the winner: Richard "The Alien" Grant. ESPN2's Bob Papa said, "So, Butler's number 8 ranking is going to take a hit." Sadly, an unsuspecting Grant was about to take a hit that he did not deserve.

As a very happy Grant raised his hands, he was approached by his opponent. Grant reached out to put an arm around Butler, but was met with an ungloved right hand to the jaw. There was no warning, no sign of what Butler was about to do.

Grant was held up by one of his trainers, and then was allowed to crumple and fall to his side in the middle of the ring with blood pouring from his mouth. Tempers flared, and officials rushed into the ring as Grant lay on his back being attended to by the ring doctors. Butler was held in the corner by referee Mike Ortega and one of his handlers as he wore a mixture of blank stare and troubled look, surveying the scene that he had just caused.

Broadcasters Atlas and Papa were outraged at what had just happened in front of them as they were signing off for the night. Papa was incensed:

> **Papa**: James Butler should never be allowed in the ring again, never. That's *assault*, that is *assault*, he should be arrested on the spot! That is assault and battery. What a *punk*!

The irony of the entire episode is that the night was a fund-raising event for victims of the 9/11 attacks in New York, labeled "Fighting for America."

> **Gravely**: As for what prompted Butler's act of poor sportsmanship, only he truly knows; however, it is worth noting that this second loss to Grant marked two defeats in a row (the other being to Ottke), and for someone

trying to work his way back up the super-middleweight ladder, it had to be a tremendous blow to his ego.

More than two years after the event, Butler commented to Tim Smith of the *New York Daily News*:

> **Butler**: I went blank. After I hit Richard everything clicked back on. It was like fist to jaw, then the noise and the lights and I could see and hear all the people. It was like I was literally brain dead for a while. If I had been thinking I would have just walked out of the ring, maybe punched a locker or broken a door or something. It wasn't planned or premeditated. It was a loss of control where my emotions just overrode everything.

The police escorted Butler out of the arena. He was later charged, and found guilty of assault and battery. Grant was able to leave the ring under his own power. He sustained a tongue laceration (that required 26 stitches to close), a dislocated jaw, loose teeth, and painful headaches.

After recovering from the attack, Grant continued to fight for about five more years, going 5–7–1 with a single no-contest, and contending (unsuccessfully) for the NABF and USBA title belts.

> **Gravely**: Butler would be escorted from the ring in handcuffs, and he eventually served four months in prison for this criminal action, as well as a temporary suspension from the New York State Athletic Commission. He was later diagnosed with bipolar disorder, and he made a not-so-stellar comeback attempt in 2004 (going 2–2). Sadly, the worst was yet to come. Almost three years after the sucker-punch fiasco, "The Harlem Hammer" took a hammer and bludgeoned Sam Kellerman, a sportswriter and boxing enthusiast, to death, putting a grotesque exclamation point on a life that had taken an unexpectedly morbid turn three years earlier.

Butler was convicted in the death of Sam Kellerman and was sentenced to 29 years and 4 months in prison for voluntary manslaughter and arson.

CHAPTER TWENTY-NINE

Don't Blink

Crawford Grimsley vs. James Thunder

March 18, 1997
Flint, Michigan

How long does it take to walk across the ring, land a punch, and count to ten? That question was answered at the IMA Sports Arena during an event aired on USA's *Tuesday Night Fights*. Al Albert and Sean O'Grady were sitting ringside when Crawford Grimsley faced James "Jimmy" Thunder in a 10-round co-main event heavyweight matchup.

At 20–1 with 18 wins by knockout, Florida's Crawford "The Terminator" Grimsley was on the rise, and with 14 of his 18 knockouts coming in the first round, he was a gunslinger with a quick draw. He started as a kickboxer, but moved into boxing and was enjoying a successful campaign to this point, having gone 12 hard rounds with George Foreman just four months earlier in Osaka, Japan. That bout was for the WBU and vacant IBA heavyweight belts. It made him even more of a prospect since he had power, *and* had withstood a 12-round assault from one of boxing's legendary punchers.

James Thunder was the boxing name for James Peau, an Australian heavyweight of Samoan descent who had come to the United States seeking to improve his skills, gain from better sparring, and put himself in line for one of the major heavyweight titles. He had held the IBO and WBF versions of the heavyweight title, but he was after one of the "big boy" versions. His record was 31–7, 25 by knockout. His impressive physique always impressed the crowds that saw him in action. I was one of the judges 2½ years earlier as he faced Mexico's

Juan Ramon "Monstro" Perez, who didn't make it out of the second round that night. Thunder was put on a fast track and had 15 fights since making his US debut, leading to this showdown of contenders. Pro boxing referee Woody Kislowski remembers the bout:

> **Kislowski**: There is a term that we use in boxing; it's an acronym. It is KTFO, which stands for really knocked out or very knocked out or something to that effect. It's a term that is applied to KOs like Jimmy Thunder's KO of Crawford Grimsley. The Thunder-Grimsley "fight" is one that will be used as an example of why a boxer should be thoroughly warmed up in the dressing room.

It was a delicious matchup of two heavy-handed fighters, one on his way up, and the other looking to remain in contention. There were questions asked about both fighters. Thunder's performance consistency was a question, and Grimsley was just not considered fully battle tested. Yes, Grimsley had gone 12 rounds with Foreman, but "Big George" was 46 years old, and nearing the end of his career. Foreman was still dangerous, but because of his age, the fight wasn't a good gauge of Grimsley place among the current heavyweight contenders. Thunder was ranked #16 by the WBC and fighting to remain in the top 20.

> **Kislowski**: Closely matched in ability, the two boxers were a virtual mirror image of each other, both big punchers, both (we thought) with good chins; Grimsley was coming off a unanimous 12-round decision loss to George Foreman for the lightly regarded IBA and WBU titles. Still, for a fighter whose opponents to that point had a combined 135–234 record, going the distance with a big puncher like Foreman indicated a pretty sturdy chin.

At the pre-fight instructions, Grimsley bounced lightly side to side as referee Monte Oswald gave the spiel. Thunder stood steady, looking down.

The bell sounded. James Thunder took two steps forward and launched an overhand right. It connected solidly to the side of Grimsley's head. Grimsley crashed down to his knees and slowly fell over, flat on his back, as the referee directed

Thunder to a neutral corner, then turned and picked up the count from the timekeeper at ringside. He kept counting all the way to ten.

> **Kislowski**: The instructions by former boxer turned referee Monte Oswald took longer than the fight. At the bell, the fighters moved toward each other and each let go with a punch, Grimsley with a left hook that missed and Thunder with a booming overhand right that didn't. Thunder's right hand landed high on Grimsley's left temple and that was all she wrote. Crawford was KTFO.

USA Network's announcing duo were shocked:

> **Albert**: ...CRACKS Grimsley with the first punch! And that looks like *it is it*!

> **O'Grady**: Over! Why is the referee counting? You don't have to count on that. This fight is over. The referee counted him out!

> **Albert**: James Thunder is known as a quick starter, but we didn't think it would be that quick. He said he had to come up with something very big, and I think he did in record fashion. James Thunder's first punch cracking Crawford Grimsley. It is over in a hurry.

Grimsley was quickly attended to. As he laid on the mat, he appeared to be throwing punches and covering up while on his back. It was a bizarre scene.

> **O'Grady**: Yeah, he's still ... look ... he's still punching, he's still trying to fight. Crawford Grimsley is confused. He's not sure what he's supposed to be doing. He's got his hands up. He thinks the fights is still ... is still going on!

Thunder was concerned about the condition of his opponent, but when Grimsley got up and appeared to be okay, they gave each other a respectful hug. Grimsley did not hang around to hear the announcement of the decision.

Ring announcer Jim Kiertzner did the math for the crowd:

> **Kiertzner**: Ladies and gentlemen. This one's over in the first round. *With* the 10-count, it lasts 13 seconds. Here's your winner, the man from Down Under, James Thunder!

The USA team just couldn't resist a final dig:

Albert: James Thunder leaves with his most memorable punch.

O'Grady: Crawford Grimsley, I think he saw thunder as well as heard thunder.

Albert: And Sean, before that knockout punch, how did you have that fight scored?

O'Grady: Well, I thought ... Grimsley was way ahead.

Grimsley fought five more times after this disappointing defeat. He went 2–2–1 to finish up his pro boxing career.

Thunder would remain a fringe contender. He fought ten more times, against top-notch opposition, going 3–7 before returning to Australia and calling it a career.

Kislowski: The next time you see a boxer who doesn't want to warm up before heading out to the ring, just show him the clip of that "fight." It won't take but a few seconds to blast the point home...

CHAPTER THIRTY

Battle Royal of Battle Royals

Riddick Bowe vs. Andrew Golota I

July 11, 1996
New York, New York

I like pro wrestling as much as the next guy, but this is one battle royal we could have done without. Referee Wayne Kelly had no idea what was in store for him. No one in the arena could have imagined what they were about to be a part of.

In Madison Square Garden, former heavyweight champion of the world Riddick "Big Daddy" Bowe (38–1, 32 KO) took on the challenge of Andrew Golota (28–0, 25 KO) in a main event bout scheduled for 12 rounds. It was not for a title, but it was a huge showdown between two of the top-five ranked heavyweights in the world.

Bowe had just "settled up" with Evander Holyfield by winning the rubber match of their famous trilogy, stopping "The Real Deal" in round 8. Golota was heading toward a title shot like a runaway freight train, mowing down opponent after opponent. The Polish powerhouse was unbeaten and considered a threat to Bowe's quest to regain his world title.

"Big Daddy" Bowe was never bigger as he entered the ring at 252 lbs., the heaviest of his career. But he was still considered the odds-on favorite on this night. Golota was angered about the fight being changed from the 10 rounds originally agreed upon to the 12 rounds that the fight became. He had considered pulling out of the fight when he learned about the change, but finally decided to go through with it after another $50,000 was added to his purse. His team entered the ring concerned about the toll such a mental weight might take on their man.

Despite over a quarter ton of boxing force in the ring, it started off as mostly a jabbing contest, both boxers wanting to establish their great jabs. Yes, they were big and powerful, but both were accomplished amateurs and Olympic medalists as well. They each had impressive records as professionals. They knew how to box as well as how to brawl.

New York boxing historian Robert Silva was in attendance with his father and has clear memories of that night:

> **Silva**: On that hot night at Madison Square Garden I didn't think Golota had a shot in hell to defeat Bowe who was coming off a tremendous 1995 in which he destroyed Herbie Hide, Jorge Gonzalez, and Evander Holyfield. Golota, I felt, was an unproven, dirty fighter. The Garden was packed that night, and my father and I were amazed how many Polish fans were there supporting their countryman. They were very loud, drunk, and vulgar. The "N word" was uttered several times throughout the evening. We were sitting in the first level behind ringside.

Excitement filled the arena as the bout got off to an interesting start, with the fighters looking strong and sharp, and exchanging crisp jabs. After the opening round, it was clear that this was not going to be an easy night for the former champion, Bowe.

> **Silva**: My father, a former amateur boxer, was irritated several times throughout the night. I kept telling him to ignore the idiots in the crowd and focus on the fight.

Round 2 saw Bowe get a warning for holding and hitting Golota behind the head. This is where Golota began working the body, with many punches straying just below Bowe's belt line and getting warnings to "keep 'em up" by referee Wayne Kelly. In the final minute of round 2, Golota was busier, but Bowe landed his share of hard shots. Golota was fighting a disciplined fight, showing great skill. If Bowe had underestimated his opponent, he now realized what he was in for.

With about 40 seconds to go in the third round, Golota landed a low left hand that earned him a warning from Kelly:

"Next time, a point. Last warning!" The big Pole continued to work and with just seconds left, he landed a right hand / left hook combination that stung Bowe. On the HBO broadcast, Larry Merchant proclaimed, "Folks, we've got a fight!"

Riddick Bowe had an all-star corner working for him: Eddie Futch was head trainer, assisted by Thell Torrance and Ralph Citro as cutman. It was apparent that this fight could turn into a need for tactical advantage to get the win, and they were clearly concerned. Golota had his own all-star team working in his corner: Roger Bloodworth, Lou Duva, and Joe Souza as cutman. There was no shortage of boxing brain power in the corners. Up to this point, the fight was close enough that the team with the better plan could have just enough of an edge; but, as the fight progressed, that would depend on their fighter's stamina and ability to stick to whatever strategy had been agreed upon. Things would soon run astray of strategy.

Round 4 saw Bowe land some heavy stuff, but about midway through the round Golota landed another combination that made Bowe stagger back into the ropes. The crowd roared with excitement as they witnessed one heck of a battle. Golota continued to land a little low every once in a while, getting repeated verbal reminders from the referee to "keep 'em up," but with 27 seconds left in the round, Golota landed a hard left hand to the groin of Bowe. In pain, he went down to a knee, and then laid on his back with his head raised up. Referee Wayne Kelly deducted one point from Golota for the infraction. Bowe had up to 5 minutes to recover, but said he could continue after only 1 minute and 22 seconds. The fight continued. The chain of events had been set into motion.

Round 5 saw Golota land some monstrous shots, snapping Bowe's head back with explosive force. Whether it was the low blow in the previous round, or the legal punishment being doled out by Golota, a change in the fight was evident as Golota had a great fifth round. Bowe's frustration showed when he gave Golota a push as he walked back to the corner.

Things slowed down in round 6, and the New York City crowd began a chant of "Let's go, Bowe!" to try and elevate the Brownsville native's intensity level. With just 28 seconds left in the round, Golota fired a low left hand that caused Bowe to bend down, grimacing and holding his groin. Referee Kelly stopped the action and ordered another point deduction from Golota's score cards. Again, Riddick Bowe had up to 5 minutes to recover, but took only 1 minute and 10 seconds before continuing. As the final seconds ticked off the clock, Golota ended the round with a solid left hook—an exclamation mark to end round 6.

Between rounds, Kelly came over to Bowe's corner to tell his cornermen to take care of some tape that was coming loose. Bowe said something about the low blows, and Kelly responded, "Riddick, you worry about the fighting. I took two points off of him, you just take care of your business."

As round 7 began, HBO's Larry Merchant said that earlier in the week, Riddick Bowe had made the remark, "Why do I have to train so hard to fight a bum?"

> **Merchant** (on why Bowe had to train so hard to fight "a bum"): He's finding out now.
>
> **Foreman**: Not only that, he's finding out how it feels to get hit below the belt. He's done a lot of that in his career.

Golota began using a double jab that seemed to freeze Bowe. With 1:54 left in the round, Golota landed another clearly low blow, prompting Kelly to stop the action and order a third point deduction. Bowe did not show any reaction to this shot, but it was clearly low. A few seconds later Bowe got a warning for throwing a rabbit punch with his right hand while his left hand was being held. Golota continued to flirt with disqualification, landing body punches at the belt line with some going slightly low. He was also landing some great shots to the body and head of Bowe, cruising to a possible victory, but how would those three lost points come into play? We would never find out, because with thirty-one seconds left in the round, as Golota was working effectively, he landed another clear and painful low blow, causing Kelly to say "That's it!" as he waved off the fight. Walking over to Riddick Bowe, who was on his back, Kelly reached down and grabbed his arm, raising it as Bowe was declared the winner. It was a disqualification win. A very interested person in attendance was former New York State Athletic Commission chairman Randy Gordon, who recalls:

> **Gordon**: The NYSAC was in disarray. Atop the commission was the chairman, Floyd Patterson, who was suffering from dementia. Running the commission was Tony Russo, Patterson's personal assistant, who had no idea how to run a commission.

Angry members of Bowe's camp entered the ring and rushed the Golota corner. Punches were thrown, and quickly the ring was filled with well over 30 people, some trying to break things up, and others fighting. Golota's trainer, Lou Duva, was injured in the melee, lying on his back apparently unconscious. People continued to storm the ring as George Foreman calmly tried to change their minds.

There was an apparent breakdown in HBO's communications system as you could hear the broadcasters commenting to each other, apparently not aware that they were still on audio. As the riot continued in the ring, and fans stood on their feet in the crowd, the broadcast continued.

Just as it appeared things were calming down, suddenly the violence erupted again on one side of the ring and spread like a wild fire throughout the arena. Punches were thrown, people were kicked. HBO's Jim Lampley appeared on screen again, this time in an upper-level location with the whole scene in the background behind him. Lampley began reporting, without a monitor to show him what was being seen by the millions tuned in around the world.

> **Lampley**: I don't know what you are seeing, because I don't have a monitor, but I can say that, in 21 years of reporting as a sports reporter and a news anchor, I've never been involved in a more personally terrifying situation than that one.

He expressed concern for 74-year-old Lou Duva who was being carried out on a stretcher with the danger swirling all around him and the EMTs who hurried him to safety.

The emotion spilled out into the crowd as fights started around the outside of the ring. There was no visible police presence to bring the situation under control.

> **Gordon**: There was little security around the ring, because the NYSAC had never thought to request more

> security from the venue, in this case, Madison Square Garden. When the skirmish began, it escalated quickly, and for several reasons:
>
> First, Bowe had given hundreds of tickets to many street kids from his hometown in Brooklyn. They erupted when Bowe went down for the final time from low blows.
>
> Second, there were hundreds of loud, inebriated fans of Golota's in the arena, and they were looking for a reason to erupt. They found their reason when Golota was DQ'd, then pounded over the head by a walkie talkie used by Bowe's corner.
>
> Third, the lack of security. In each fighter's corner stood a single security guard. Each looked to be at least 70 years of age and completely out of shape.

There were quite a few gentlemen in suit and tie, probably officials with the state athletic commission, but uniformed officers were nowhere to be found. The situation was treated like a forest fire: just let it burn itself out.

> **Silva**: Golota dominated Bowe from the opening bell. Other than the blatant low blows, Golota could do no wrong. He out-jabbed Bowe, which shocked us because Bowe had one of the greatest jabs of his era. Bowe did not train for this fight and he took a horrific beating. Finally, after referee Wayne Kelly DQ'd Golota for landing a lethal combination to Bowe's private parts, the Polish fans behind us were cursing up a storm at his decision. Then, when Bowe's security guard hit Golota over the head with a walkie talkie, the Garden began to riot. It was a race riot. Black fans fighting the Polish fans. I grabbed my father and took him by the concession stands while my eyes couldn't believe what I was seeing. I mean, it was an all-out race riot that went on for 15-20 minutes. Grown men beating the hell out of each other because of what happened in the ring. Beer and objects were flying. Men were getting slammed on top of chairs.

Golota's crew had been directed to the locker room area, while Riddick Bowe was led out by a group of people tightly surrounding the big man, and walking him back to the locker room as he surveyed the situation with a frustrated look on his face.

As HBO's Jim Lampley signed off from the broadcast, there were some live shots around the closing credits which did show uniformed police officers starting to regain control of the crowd.

> **Silva**: It took us over an hour to get out of the Garden. I waited until there were a few fans left to get my father out of there. My father had an explosive temper, and he would've gotten into a fight with one of the Polish fans if they even looked at him cross-eyed. I was concerned about Lou Duva, as he suffered a heart attack while the riot was going on.

> **Gordon**: Guns were fired. Bottles and chairs were thrown. Rows of chairs were overturned. Exits were blocked by overturned chairs, fighting fans, and fallen bodies. People were on the floor, bleeding and screaming. I took my wife, Roni, by the hand, and made my way toward the closest exit. It was blocked. We continued to turn and look around. By constantly turning, we avoided several chairs which were tossed our way. We were set to go under the ring when we saw an exit across the room open up, as fighting fans deserted the area to fight elsewhere. We ran for the exit and made it.

It was reported that 22 people were injured during the event, and 16 were arrested. Bowe's manager, Rock Newman, received a one-year suspension, and was fined $250,000 by the New York State Athletic Commission.

> **Gordon**: Once safely in the back, Roni burst into tears. To this day, it remains as the scariest event of our lives. I put all the blame on then New York governor George Pataki who, by ripping the NYSAC apart after his defeat of Mario Cuomo two years earlier, weakened the commission to the point nobody there knew what they were doing, and had no clue that additional security would be needed.

In spite of what happened on this night, a rematch was made, and took place five months later in Atlantic City.

CHAPTER THIRTY-ONE

What's Your Name?

Samson Cohen vs. Chavez Francisco

May 1, 1995
Johnson City, Tennessee

Ring announcer Thomas Treiber, then 21 years old, may still have nightmares about this night in Freedom Hall, broadcast on ESPN2. The event featured a WBF featherweight title bout.

> **Treiber**: It landed on a best-of-sports bloopers tape and even Marv Albert used the blooper as a guest on David Letterman's show. It was only my second or third time on national TV.

So what was this event that helped to shape the career of one of boxing's premiere ring announcers? It occurred during a 6-round cruiserweight undercard bout between South Carolina's Samson Cohen and local boy Chavez Francisco.

Francisco was tall and muscular. His opponent, sporting a short-cropped Mohawk haircut, was shorter but aggressive, knowing that he had to find a way inside the long reach of the taller Francisco. That fight plan paid dividends just 12 seconds into the first round as he was able to connect with a short right hook that sent Francisco to the mat, landing on one knee. Francisco sprang right up, not appearing to be hurt, and the bell sounded to end the first round.

In round 2, Cohen's straight-ahead attack continued to work as he was able to land some good shots, but at about the halfway point of the round, Francisco started to zero in on his target, and began landing more shots of his own.

The two started off round 3 with no concern about defense. They wailed away on each other. Cohen went down in one of the corners, but the referee ruled it a slip and ordered a cornerman to wipe up the excess water on the mat there. As the action continued, Francisco landed a solid right hand to the mid-section, and Cohen went down, taking a hard left hand shot on his way down. He claimed a low blow, and the referee took his word for it.

The referee allowed Cohen to take up to 5 minutes. In addition, he allowed Cohen's cornermen to refresh him and give him instructions as he sat on a stool inside the ring.

As Cohen rested on the stool and got instructions from his trainer, the ESPN2 replay showed that it was clearly a right hand to the body, a legal, clean punch, that sent him down.

The ESPN2 broadcast team of Tony Paige and Bob Varsha found it an unusual scene:

> **Varsha**: (laughing) Now his corner is out there working on him.
>
> **Paige**: (laughing) That's weird, you're not supposed to do that. You're supposed to give him as much time as he needs, I believe up to 5 minutes to recuperate. But, it's not to put ice, and water, and give instructions.

Chavez Francisco went over to his corner to rinse his mouth with water, and was ordered back to the neutral corner by the referee.

> **Paige**: (chuckling) I mean, if Samson can get some advice, then so should Chavez.
>
> **Varsha**: No question.
>
> **Paige**: Ah, they're making it up as we go along.

After 2 minutes and 40 seconds of break time, the referee called them back to action.

> **Varsha**: Alright, we'll pick up the round.
>
> **Paige**: *Strange* round, Bob.
>
> **Varsha**: *Very* unusual.

If Cohen was injured by that low blow, he recovered very fast as he came out and staggered Francisco with a right hand to the chin. Francisco then turned things around, sending Cohen down with another solid body shot. Cohen was on the ground telling the referee that it was a low blow, but the ref wasn't buying it this time, and started the count. Cohen's corner began yelling at him to get up, and he did. Francisco jumped at Cohen, trying to put him down again with combination punching, but the bell rang to end this crazy third round.

The fourth round started with the two brawling. The referee nearly fell as he tried to get between them and give admonishments to both fighters for not breaking clean on command. It was getting down and dirty with lots of clinching, rabbit punches, and kidney punches. The crowd had thinned out as many had left after the main event title fight, but the few spectators that remained were really into it, as Francisco landed a series of punches right before the bell to end the round.

As the broadcast returned from the commercial break, Paige and Varsha remarked (over a slow-motion replay of the action):

> **Varsha**: Here's another look at some of the action, of what has been a very entertaining, but hardly conventional prize fight.
>
> **Paige**: It's trench warfare. They continued well after the bell.
>
> **Varsha**: I think Wayne Stoffel, the referee, didn't hear the bell, and allowed the fighters to stay with it. The crowd went crazy.

Round 5 continued the action from the previous round, with both fighters loading up with wild punches, but Cohen was getting the worse end of the deal. With Cohen appearing softened up and ready to go, Francisco landed a crushing right hand to the side of Cohen's head that sent him down to one knee. He beat the count, but didn't want any more punishment, and the referee waved it to a stop.

> **Varsha**: That was a strange one. Two controversial knockdowns. Lots of punches thrown, and landed.

As the broadcast returned from commercial break, ring announcer Thomas Treiber was in the ring:

> **Treiber**: ...with a time of 1 minute, 45 seconds of the fifth round, referee Wayne Stoffel stops this bout, with your winner by technical knockout, here's...

And the microphone picked him up as he paused awkwardly, looked confused, and walked over to the winner and said in a whispered tone "What's your name?"

The boxer apparently did not understand what Treiber was asking him, and gave him just his first name, "Chavez."

The crowd laughed and hooted as Treiber looked up with an embarrassed facial expression.

> **Treiber**: Here's ... Chav-ez.

Broadcaster Bob Varsha tried to come to the poor ring announcer's aid with a bit of levity:

> **Varsha**: Chav-ezzzzzz Frannnnnnn-cisco! We try to help out where we can here on the Deuce. Ah, it happens to all of us, Thomas.

Thomas Treiber remembers it vividly:

> **Treiber**: The fight ended by stoppage so I grabbed my mic and entered the ring. After getting the official time of stoppage, I realized that I had left my card ringside with the names on it. However, the second I did, the floor director was cueing me frantically to announce the winner, so I started the announcement with the time and then had to ask the winning fighter his name (which could be heard on the mic) causing laughter from the crowd. It was a lonely night in Johnson City as I felt humiliated and that my career was over. However, it ended up becoming a great learning experience, and after an encouraging phone call from the promoter, Larry Carrier, I was given the opportunity to do the next ESPN show that he did. The only way to get good at something is to learn from your mistakes and move forward.

Learning experience indeed. Treiber has gone on to become one of boxing's most sought-after ring announcers, working national and global events for Showtime, HBO, ESPN's *Friday Night Fights*, CBS, Fox Sports Net, Comcast Sports Net, USA Network, Sky Sports, ITV, and pay-per-views.

CHAPTER THIRTY-TWO

Could It Happen Again?

Riddick Bowe vs. Andrew Golota II

December 14, 1996
Atlantic City, New Jersey

After all that went down in their first meeting, it seemed unlikely that a rematch would occur, but just five months later, at the Atlantic City Convention Center, Riddick Bowe and Andrew Golota picked up where they had left off in Madison Square Garden.

The bout was again broadcast on HBO. Eddie Cotton got the call to referee this bout, and it was a very high-profile assignment considering what had happened when these two fighters last met. There was a big police presence in place this time. Confidence was high that there would not be a repeat of the violence which erupted following their first meeting.

Bowe came into the ring to Bruce Springsteen's "Born in the USA." He knew he could not under-estimate his opponent this time, and that was apparent as he had trimmed 17 pounds off of his weight from the last fight, tipping the scale at 235 lbs. Golota would actually outweigh Bowe this time around, coming in at 239 lbs.

The bout started with a first round that saw Golota use a sharp double jab to keep Bowe at bay. The same pattern that developed in the first meeting was being established.

About 2 minutes into the second round, Bowe was caught with a right/left combination that sent him to the canvas. When he got up he was immediately under assault by Golota, who moved him back into a corner where Bowe tried to fight back but got caught with more heavy shots. With thirty seconds left in the round, Golota banged Bowe with a head butt, prompting the referee to stop the action and tell the judges to deduct one point for the flagrant foul. The time for the point deduction did two things for Bowe: it took a point away from Golota's score, but also gave Bowe just a few more seconds to recover from the punishment he had suffered. The round finished with Bowe again leaning against the ropes in the corner and Golota pressing him. Between rounds, it was discovered that Golota had a bad gash over his left eye, probably from the head butt.

Bowe did not have trainer Eddie Futch in his corner this time around. Futch had reportedly stated that Bowe was a "lost cause" and would not train him for this fight. Bowe was still in good hands with Thell Torrence, who had moved up to the head trainer position.

Round 3 saw the cut over Golota's eye start to bleed quite a bit, and Bowe smartly began targeting that eye. The two exchanged hard shots throughout the round, but Bowe seemed to regain a little momentum and confidence.

Round 4 was big for Riddick Bowe, who landed a right hand and an uppercut that hurt Golota badly. Bowe pressed the advantage and sent his opponent down for what was the first knockdown ever suffered by Andrew Golota. He rose up with blood dripping down from the cut over the left eye and looked to be in bad shape. Bowe went after him, and Golota resorted to an old game plan, what seemed to be his natural instinct: low blows. Cotton showed restraint by calling time, taking Golota aside to give him a stern and clear warning about the low blows, and letting the bout continue. It was a good strategy for Golota, who gained a few precious seconds to clear his head from the knockdown. But, with just 40 seconds left in the round, Golota gave in to that voice inside his head and landed a low blow combination that sent Bowe to the mat. The referee called time and instructed the judges to deduct 1 point from Golota. He gave Bowe up to 5 minutes to recover, but Bowe used only 53 seconds before telling Cotton that he was ready to re-engage. The round ended, and Golota returned to his corner to be given clear and precise instructions from trainer Roger Bloodworth: "No more body punches!" It was clear that Andrew's corner could see where things were headed.

The two came out for round 5 looking spent, but they fought as if they had an agreement to trade power shots. Bowe was staggered with a right hand, followed up by some body punches that sent him face down to the canvas. Bowe got up at about 7 seconds into the count, was asked if he could continue, nodded yes, and was allowed to resume the fight. He spent the last 30 seconds of the round leaning against the ropes bravely trying to survive, and survive he did, but paid a terrible price to do so.

The sixth round saw Bowe start off by taking steps backward and laying on the ropes with Golota's jab pushing him back. Forty seconds into the round, Golota landed a rabbit punch and the action was halted as the referee admonished him for the tactic. Bowe was now standing in the center of the ring, staying off of the ropes and actually walking Golota back into a corner. The two exchanged punches for the remainder of the round in what was a grueling test for both fighters. In between rounds, a close-up shot revealed what looked like a hole just below the mouth of Golota, a very deep wound. With that, and the cut over the eye, Golota looked the worse for wear, but Bowe had taken the kind of punishment that can be longer lasting for a boxing career. This was a brutal one. Both corners were pleading with their fighters to fight through it, to outlast the other. It was like a jockey going to the whip in a horse race, but jockeys do that in the home stretch, and this was only round 7 of a fight scheduled for 10 rounds.

Bowe was willing to stand in the middle of the ring and trade with Golota, but it was Golota who looked steadier on his feet, eventually driving Bowe back into the ropes again. It seemed that Bowe was just one punch away from being stopped throughout the round, but he survived. Between rounds, Thell Torrence told him: "If you don't show me something this round, I'm going to stop it."

It seemed that Bowe was just floating in the water during round 8, looking worn, spent, and empty. He managed to show a spark of life and landed two solid right hands, but it was about all he could muster. Meanwhile, Golota's pace slowed and he was not able to summon the strength to sustain a finishing attack. As Bowe wobbled back to his corner, it seemed hopeless, but his champion's pride kept him going.

To start round 9, Bowe looked so worn out that he threw a combination and nearly stumbled backwards as his legs betrayed him. With Bowe reclining in the corner again, Golota stepped in and was surprised by a quick right hand that made him step back. Bowe was out of gas, but still dangerous enough to keep Golota from going all-out to finish him. Golota was still in control of the fight, and inexplicably, he unleashed a three-punch combination to the groin of Bowe. There was no reason for it, no accident, just three hard punches where they didn't belong. Bowe went down on his back, in pain. The referee stopped the action, and after a few seconds of confusion, called a halt to the fight at 2:58 of round 9. The winner was Riddick Bowe. Punished, beaten down, emptied of all the fire he entered the ring with, yet the victor.

Michael Buffer announced the decision. This time, no one rushed Golota's corner, no one entered the ring, thanks to a very visible police presence that kept a lid on any potential violence.

Why would a professional fighter who spends his life training and preparing himself to perform well enough to become champion of the world do something like this, not once, but twice, and when he was so close to scoring an upset against a man who would go on to be inducted into the boxing hall of fame? It's doubtful that even Golota himself knows the answer. After the referee waved off the fight, Golota's trainer, Lou Duva, walked up to him yelling, and Golota was heard, sobbing, "I stupid. I stupid." After these two displays, Golota earned the sub-nickname "The Foul Pole."

New York boxing historian Robert Silva felt that Bowe lost by winning:

> **Silva:** I was hoping there would be a rematch as I felt a focused and well-trained Bowe would get his revenge. Unfortunately, he took an even more severe beating in the rematch. He won both fights by DQ, but he was never the same physically and mentally afterward.

Golota fought on for over 16 years. In fact, his very next fight saw him in a WBC world title challenge against Lennox Lewis where he was stopped in the first round. Golota fought

22 fights after his final encounter with Riddick Bowe, mostly against top-quality opposition, including three unsuccessful world title challenges, an NABF title challenge, and some fights for minor titles. He went 13–7–1 with a single no-contest after facing Bowe for the second time.

Riddick Bowe was never the same. He stepped away from the game and returned nearly eight years later to fight three more times, though against journeymen. He won those bouts, but never fought for another title.

APPENDIX

Boxing Nicknames

Part of the color of the sport of boxing are the nicknames given to and adopted by professional boxers. Let's test your boxing IQ (no cheating now!). Some of these names were used by more than one high-profile boxer. How many of these 50 nicknames ring a bell? Get them all and you're a boxing guru!

THE ANIMAL

CANELO

THE BEAST

VAMPIRE

THE PAZMANIAN DEVIL

THE GREATEST

SMOKIN'

CHAPO

HALF MAN—HALF AMAZING

THE QUIET MAN

THE REAL DEAL

BIG DADDY

MI VIDA LOCA

HANDS OF STONE

LITTLE HANDS OF STONE

CHICANITO

THE BODY SNATCHER

THE POCKET ROCKET

THE MAGICIAN

SCHOOL BOY

MACHO
BOOM BOOM
ICE-T
THE HAWK
LIGHTS OUT
THE HIT MAN
LITTLE HANDS OF STEEL
MARVELOUS
BUMP CITY
THE GOLDEN BOY
LITTLE RED
MOTOR CITY
THE DARK DESTROYER
THE EASTON ASSASIN
MAROMERO
THE LONE STAR COBRA
SWEET PEA
THE BLADE
THE BLACK MAMBA
FEARLESS
EL TORITO
QUICKSILVER
NO DOUBT
THE FLEA
THE BRONX BOMBER
THE SQUIRREL
THE EASTERN BEAST
THE SAN FERNANDO HAMMER
THE PINK CAT
THE PUNCHING POSTMAN

Acknowledgments

For their support and contributions, I gratefully acknowledge:

- My wife, Tammy: thank you for all of your love and support with this project. I look forward to many more nights of eating peanuts and popcorn, watching the "big fights" together.
- My daughter, Monica: I'm so proud of you. Thanks for going to boxing and kickboxing with me.
- My son, Daniel. Dad's still enjoying boxing, just like you would want him to.
- My dad, John: thanks for all of the fun we've had going to "the fights" and watching them together on television.
- My brother, Thomas: a real "boxing fan" (it's in the blood).
- My publisher, Bob McLain: Pulp Hero Press is a knockout!
- My friend Mike Weaver: I can't thank you enough for being part of my first boxing book. I enjoyed your career as a fan, and never imagined that you would write the foreword for my book one day.

A "shout out" to my three favorite boxing podcasts:

- In The Corner Boxing Radio (Lee Harris & Charlie Elwood)
- World Championship Boxing Podcast (Logan "Time-Traveler" and Robert "1" Silva)
- Fight Heads Live (Ramon "R.L." Malpica)

And to my dear friends and acquaintances in the boxing community. There are so many wonderful people that have shared our love of boxing. I treasure my relationship with each of you. Thank you!

Above all:

My Lord and Savior—Jesus Christ.

Romans 10:13.

About the Author

Boxing historian Dan Sisneros was a professional boxing judge with the New Mexico State Athletic Commission during the 1990s. He was a featured writer for *Pro Boxing Update/Flash*, and hosted his own boxing show on Albuquerque's public access television (*The 8-Count Boxing Hour*) as well as co-hosting *Rising Stars Boxing* with Henry Tafoya which aired on New Mexico's CBS & WB stations statewide.

Dan has built one of the largest collections of boxing matches on videotape/DVD in the world. His boxing-on-video service has been used by many of the biggest names in the sport to prepare for upcoming bouts. He is an editor at Boxrec.com and contributed videotape footage used in the HBO documentary *TAPIA* about the life of his friend, world champion Johnny "Mi Vida Loca" Tapia.

Dan is also the creator/administrator of the Classic Boxing group on Facebook where boxing fans can share their thoughts and experiences about this great sport. In addition, Dan's blog, *The Boxing Guru's Hall of Fame* (guruofboxing. blogspot.com) honors the lesser-known, but no less awesome, warriors of professional boxing.

Dan grew up in Southeast Los Angeles, and now lives with his wife, Tammy, in southern New Mexico where he is enjoying retirement and being a grandfather to two awesome granddaughters. If you would like to talk boxing, contact him via e-mail at: disneyguru@outlook.com.

About the Contributors

Thanks to each of you who submitted memories of some crazy nights in boxing!

HENRY ANAYA JR was a world-ranked contender in the late 1980s and early 90s. He is the older brother of Charles "Poison" Anaya, and a member of the New Mexico Boxing Hall of Fame. (boxrec.com/en/boxer/4000)

JOE ANTONACCI is recognized as one of boxing's top ring announcers. He has announced for almost every major network that carries televised boxing.

BRAD BERKWITT is the author of *Boxing Interviews of a Lifetime* and is the CEO/publisher of RingsideReport.com.

LOUIE BURKE was a world-ranked lightweight contender in the 1980s. His two fights with Freddie Roach are the stuff legends are made of. He was the ESPN champion, has served as a member of the New Mexico State Athletic Commission, and is one of boxing's top trainers. Louie has also been inducted into the California; El Paso, Texas; and New Mexico Boxing halls of fame. (boxrec.com/en/boxer/2880)

DAN CUSHNER has trained both amateur and professional boxers. He has promoted, worked corners, and was called "the best damn cutman in New Mexico" by none other than the light-heavyweight champion of the world and boxing hall-of-famer, Bob Foster.

VIC DE WYSOCKI has worked over 200 bouts as a professional boxing referee, and over 100 as a judge. He has been an official for over ten years, and is an editor with BoxRec.com (boxrec.com/en/referee/409134)

RANDY GORDON is the former chairman of the New York State Athletic Commission. He has done broadcasting of boxing events over the years, served as editor-in-chief of *The Ring* magazine and *Boxing Illustrated*, and hosts *At the Fights* with former heavyweight contender Gerry Cooney on Sirius XM Radio. He was inducted into the New Jersey Boxing Hall of Fame in 2005, and the New York Boxing Hall of Fame in 2016. (njboxinghof.org/randy-gordon)

VERNON GRAVELY is a freelance writer who contributed to *The Ring* magazine (back in the '90s). He recently (in 2016) completed his first video documentary, *Death of a Champion, Birth of a Rule: The Tony Marino Story*, about the 1930s bantamweight champ whose death inspired the three-knockdown rule.

LEE GROVES is a writer/resident historian at RingTV, a feature writer for *The Ring* magazine, an International Boxing Hall of Fame voter, the author of *Tales from the Vault: A Celebration of 100 Boxing Closet Classics*, and a punch counter/writer/analyst/researcher at CompuBox.

MARVIN JONES was born in Tennessee, but now resides and fights out of Puerto Rico where he works with local youth through his boxing program. (boxrec.com/en/boxer/370929)

WOODY KISLOWSKI has worked over 100 bouts as a referee, and nearly 200 as a judge over his 20 years as an official. (boxrec.com/en/referee/401479)

RICH LAMONTAGNE was a fan favorite. He campaigned in the cruiserweight division and produced some memorable bouts during the thirty-seven fights of his professional career. (boxrec.com/en/boxer/7613)

RUDY LOVATO faced many of the top names in the sport during his long career. He was a New Mexico local favorite as both a boxer and a kickboxer. (boxrec.com/en/boxer/7391)

SANDY MARTINEZ-PINO has been involved in amateur and professional boxing for many years, and has served as a judge and a member of the New Mexico State Athletic Commission. (boxrec.com/en/judge/465626)

NATHAN PALMER is a pro boxing judge with over 800 bouts worked, including several WBC World title fights. He is a boxing historian and editor with BoxRec.com. (boxrec.com/en/judge/401080)

DANIEL PEREZ was a world-ranked middleweight and light-heavyweight. He challenged Nigel Benn for the WBC super-middleweight title in 1995. (boxrec.com/en/boxer/4436)

CARLO PINEDA, known as "Mr. Body Shots," is a boxing enthusiast/connoisseur, boxing video collector, and former member of the Los Angeles boxing media as editor and writer for the Boxing Jungle website.

RENE RAMIREZ is a huge boxing fan, and the creator/administrator of the Fight Group on Facebook (facebook.com/groups/thefightfroup).

ROBERT SILVA is one of boxing's top historians. He co-hosts the World Championship Boxing Podcast. (blogtalkradio.com/world-championship-boxing)

BOB SPAGNOLA has represented many of the top names in professional boxing over the years as president of Bad Boyz Inc. He has also done broadcasting of many televised boxing events.

THOMAS TREIBER is an internationally known ring announcer for professional boxing, mixed martial arts, K-1, and professional wrestling. Throughout his 20-year career he has worked in Japan, England, Kazakhstan, Uruguay, Mexico, Puerto Rico, Dominican Republic, Northern Ireland, Canada, and the United States. (thomastreiber.com)

MIKE WEAVER: Mike is the WBA former heavyweight champion of the world. His miraculous one-punch knockout in the 15th round of "Big" John Tate to win the title is one of boxing's legends. (boxrec.com/en/boxer/405)

RYAN WISSOW was a professional boxer and is now president of the Women's International Boxing Association. (boxrec.com/en/boxer/15820)

Printed in Great Britain
by Amazon